the comfort table

RECIPES FOR EVERYDAY OCCASIONS

KATIE LEE

photography by miki duisterhof

Simon Spotlight Entertainment
A Division of Simon & Schuster, Inc.
1230 Avenue of the Americas
New York, NY 10020

First Simon Spotlight Entertainment hardcover
edition October 2009

SIMON SPOTLIGHT ENTERTAINMENT and colophon are
trademarks of Simon & Schuster, Inc.

For information about special discounts for bulk purchases, please contact
Simon & Schuster Special Sales at 1-866-506-1949 or business@simonandschuster.com.

The Simon & Schuster Speakers Bureau can bring authors to your live event. For
more information or to book an event contact the Simon & Schuster Speakers
Bureau at 1-866-248-3049 or visit our website at www.simonspeakers.com.

Designed by Jane Archer/www.psbella.com

Manufactured in the United States of America

10 9 8 7 6 5 4 3 2 1

Library of Congress Cataloging-in-Publication Data

Lee, Katie, 1981–
  The comfort table : recipes for everyday occasions / Katie Lee.
      p. cm.
   ISBN-13 978-1-4391-2674-5
 1. Cookery, American. I. Title.
   TX715.J5936 2009
   641.5973—dc22   2009025267

**to mom
and grandma—**

women who taught me
that being a good hostess
isn't just about the food that
you serve, but how you
make people feel
in your home

contents

introduction

When I started writing my first cookbook,

The Comfort Table, I was so excited to share my recipes and thoughts on food with all of you. My grandmother sent me her recipe box, my great-aunt shared a couple of her recipes with me, and so did a few friends. During the writing process, I found myself not only on a culinary adventure, but also on an emotional journey through the foods of my past. Food has a nostalgic power; just like when you hear a song and it takes you back to a certain time in your life, cooking and eating can transport you to a moment in time. The majority of my warmest memories are of time spent around the table with those who I love.

I think it's safe to say that in the time between writing that first book and the publication of this second edition, the world we live in is a different place. Jobs have been lost, homes foreclosed, and cars repossessed. Everyone has been affected in some capacity and many people are struggling to make ends meet.

By no means did I grow up in a wealthy family. I'm from a small town in West Virginia called Milton (population: 2,387). My mom and I lived in the same neighborhood as my grandparents, great-grandmother, and great-aunt and uncle. I always had family around, and while we didn't have money, we did have the most important thing: each other. I never felt like I wanted for a thing and I didn't know that there was anything that I was missing out on. And while my life in New York City now may be very different from my childhood in West Virginia, some things have always remained a constant in my life—family, love, food, and my love of food.

Writing *Recipes for Everyday Occasions* has been somewhat of an evolution. I started with the idea of writing menus for holidays and celebrations, but the more things around me changed, the less I thought that it needed to be a special occasion to share a meal with family and friends. Isn't every day a gift and reason enough to enjoy yourself? In a time like this, we find comfort in one another's support and also in the food that we are eating. It's called "comfort food" for a reason. Some of the most fun I've had with friends hasn't been at an extravagant party, but on a Sunday afternoon eating fried chicken and a big slice of chocolate banana cream pie, or lighting a fire and having a pot roast and buttered noodles on the first snowy day of the season.

My friends know that I adore entertaining and I'll take any excuse to have a get-together. Whether it's a summer barbecue, a fall harvest dinner, a cocktail party, or our annual Chrismukkah shindig, I'm always planning something. I feel my best when I'm cooking for those I love, and having them in my home is such a treat. The most important thing my grandma taught me about being a hostess is that it isn't just about the food—it's mostly about the way you make people feel in your home. If you put the words "comfort" and "table" together, it spells "comfortable," and that's what it's all about.

Great food, company, laughter, all the while making memories—to me, you can't put a price on it. These are the times that are important in life, these everyday occasions.

my must-haves

My house practically has a revolving door. There are always friends knocking and they are usually hungry. These are items that I always have on standby, because I never know when I might find myself having an everyday occasion.

HERBS

I prefer to use fresh herbs, but dried are good to keep on hand for use in a pinch. I recommend planting a small herb garden either in your yard or in a window box.

my essentials

BASIL
CHIVES
CILANTRO
FLAT-LEAF PARSLEY
MINT
OREGANO
ROSEMARY
TARRAGON
THYME

SPICES

I have a whole shelf in my pantry devoted to spices. Each is labeled with the date that I opened it, and after six months, I throw it away and buy a new one. The potency diminishes—I like to be sure my spices are very flavorful. Whenever I travel, I pick up spices to re-create the dishes I ate on vacation when I get home.

my essentials

BAY LEAVES
CHINESE FIVE-SPICE
CHILI POWDER
GROUND CLOVES
GROUND CUMIN
PAPRIKA
CREOLE SEASONING
GROUND CINNAMON
CINNAMON STICKS
CRUSHED RED PEPPER FLAKES
BLACK PEPPERCORNS
GROUND GINGER
GROUND NUTMEG
GARLIC POWDER
GARLIC SALT
CELERY SALT
SESAME SEEDS
ONION POWDER
DRY MUSTARD
VANILLA EXTRACT
VANILLA BEANS
ZA'TAR

IN THE **FREEZER**

Fresh veggies and fruits are best, but I always keep some in my freezer. Frozen vegetables are good to cook a quick soup; frozen fruits are ideal for smoothies or to add to mixed drinks, or to make a sauce for ice cream.

IN THE **REFRIGERATOR**

Some people say you can tell everything you need to know about a person by their shoes, I say look in their refrigerator. My meals are never the same from day to day, but there are some must-haves that I always keep on hand. I like to have the makings for panini or to be able to throw together a quick cheese plate for drop-in guests. And I always, always have a bottle of Champagne chilled and ready to go!

my essentials

PEAS

CORN

PEARL ONIONS

EDAMAME

STRAWBERRIES

RASPBERRIES

BLACKBERRIES

CHERRIES

MANGO

PAPAYA

HOMEMADE CHICKEN STOCK

HOMEMADE PESTO
(frozen in ice cube trays)

PIZZA DOUGH

HOMEMADE COOKIE DOUGH
(for slicing and baking)

ICE CREAM

my essentials

MILK

UNSALTED BUTTER

PLAIN YOGURT

HEAVY CREAM

SOUR CREAM

CREAM CHEESE

CHEESE (goat, Brie, cheddar, blue,
Parmesan, Gorgonzola, ricotta)

JARRED ARTICHOKE HEARTS

JARRED ROASTED RED
BELL PEPPERS

HUMMUS

OLIVES

JAMS

MUSTARD (yellow, Dijon, and honey)

KETCHUP

MAYONNAISE

HOT SAUCES

PREPARED HORSERADISH

CITRUS (lemons, limes, oranges)

FRESH FRUITS, VEGETABLES,
AND SALAD GREENS

CHAMPAGNE

IN THE **PANTRY**

A well-stocked pantry is a time saver. Not having to run to the grocery store for every little thing at the last minute makes a big difference when the urge to cook strikes.

IN THE **BAR**

It's cocktail hour somewhere! And having a versatile bar makes it that much more fun when guests arrive. In addition to spirits and mixers, it's a great idea to keep a drink-mixing guide by the bar in case someone requests a cocktail you're not familiar with.

my essentials

BOURBON

VODKA

LIGHT RUM

GIN

TEQUILA

VERMOUTH

MIXERS
(tonic, seltzer, juices)

TOOLS
(ice bucket and tongs, shaker, strainer, two-sided jigger, bottle opener)

HORS D'OEUVRES ON THE FLY

If I'm having friends over for drinks last minute, these are my go-to hors d'oeuvres. They take only minutes to prepare and are always a hit and appropriate for any occasion.

- Wrap store-bought breadsticks in prosciutto.

- Fill endive leaves with hummus and dust with paprika. (Endive leaves make great vessels for other simple, tasty combinations as well, like goat cheese with crushed walnuts and drizzled with honey, or smoked salmon with crème fraîche and chives.)

- Make a variety of crostini by toasting thinly sliced baguettes and topping with goat cheese and roasted red pepper, Gorgonzola and fig jam, ricotta with olive oil and sea salt, or olive tapenade.

- Marinate olives with fresh herbs and red pepper flakes.

- Season nuts with chili powder and toast lightly.

PARTY TIPS

- Make lists, lists, and more lists of everything that needs to be done for the party.

- Clean and set up the party space the day before.

- To save space, move any nonessential furniture out of the party area and into your bedroom.

- Stash old mail, magazines, and any other loose papers in decorative tins or baskets out of eyesight.

- Take some time to tidy up your bathroom. Clear your sink of beauty product clutter, put out fresh soap, clean hand towels, and plenty of toilet paper.

- Short on space? Clear off the shelf of a bookcase and use for bar setup with martini and wine glasses, a couple of drink garnishes, and plenty of cocktail napkins.

- Designated drivers and nondrinkers shouldn't be forced to drink water all night. Offer a nonalcoholic drink such as a fruit spritzer. Just mix fruit juice, club soda, and sliced fruit.

- To break the ice, give an outgoing friend a tray of hors d'oeuvres to pass around, and put another friend on drink duty.

- When it's time to wrap up the party, turn the lights up and put away the booze.

fall harvest dinner

I love every season, but there really is something special about fall. When I was a little girl, I'd ride the school bus home and watch the maple trees in my grandparents' yard turn colors. Each afternoon, as the bus turned the corner onto their street, I'd anticipate the changing leaves as they went from green, to yellow, to a deep orange before falling from the branches. My grandpa would rake the fallen leaves into giant piles for me and my friends to play in.

Fall also brings a bounty of beautiful produce. I especially love the rustic flavors of squash, pumpkins, and root vegetables. Here in New York, we get the most wonderful varieties of apples. I like to take a drive north of the city to the orchards and load up on apples and cider. With its rich autumnal colors and textures, this menu incorporates all of my favorite fall flavors and turns each plate into a delicious cornucopia.

MENU

PICKLED VEGETABLES

ROASTED PUMPKIN
AND POMEGRANATE SALAD

DIJON BRUSSELS SPROUTS

CHICKEN WITH MUSHROOMS AND GARLIC

HARD APPLE CIDER

RUSTIC APPLE PIE

SERVES 6

WINE

White Bordeaux

PLAYLIST

"Boys with Girlfriends" • BY MEIKO
"You Are the Best Thing" • BY RAY LA MONTAGNE
"Taylor" • BY JACK JOHNSON
"1234" • BY FEIST
"Back Together" • BY CITIZEN COPE

pickled vegetables

I am a vinegar lover, so anything pickled is a favorite of mine. I make pickled vegetables throughout the year. This recipe calls for carrots, cauliflower, red peppers, and jalapeños, but try substituting other vegetables you enjoy in different seasons.

In a nonreactive stockpot over medium-high heat, bring the vinegar, water, sugar, salt, peppercorns, and bay leaf to a boil, stirring until the sugar dissolves. Add the vegetables and reduce heat to a simmer. Cook until the vegetables are tender, 10 to 12 minutes. Remove from the heat and let cool completely. Transfer to an airtight container and refrigerate until serving. Drain before serving. (Keeps about 2 weeks.)

6 SERVINGS (6 CUPS)
PREP TIME: 15 MINUTES
INACTIVE PREP TIME: 2 HOURS TO COOL
COOK TIME: 12 TO 15 MINUTES

$2\frac{1}{2}$ CUPS APPLE CIDER VINEGAR

$2\frac{1}{2}$ CUPS WATER

$\frac{1}{4}$ CUP SUGAR

2 TEASPOONS KOSHER SALT

1 TEASPOON BLACK PEPPERCORNS

1 BAY LEAF

2 CUPS BABY CARROTS

1 HEAD CAULIFLOWER, BROKEN INTO BITE-SIZE FLORETS

2 RED BELL PEPPERS, CUT INTO STRIPS

2 JALAPEÑOS, CUT LENGTHWISE INTO QUARTERS AND SEEDED (OR LEAVE SEEDS FOR SPICIER PICKLES)

TIP

These pickled vegetables make great hostess gifts and party favors.

roasted pumpkin and pomegranate salad

Last fall I was writing pumpkin recipes for a segment on the CBS *Early Show*. Most of my pumpkin dishes use canned pumpkin puree and I wanted to come up with a recipe that made use of fresh pumpkin since it was in season. Using fresh pumpkin is much easier than it looks, and tastes so good. This salad has a very festive and colorful look with the deep orange pumpkin, bright red pomegranate seeds, and dark green arugula. It certainly found a permanent place on my fall menu.

For the salad

3 CUPS SUGAR PUMPKIN, PEELED AND CUT INTO ½-INCH CUBES (ABOUT 3 POUNDS)

2 TABLESPOONS OLIVE OIL

KOSHER SALT AND FRESHLY GROUND BLACK PEPPER

6 CUPS LIGHTLY PACKED BABY ARUGULA

2 TABLESPOONS ROASTED AND SALTED PEPITAS (SHELLED PUMPKIN SEEDS)

SEEDS OF 1 POMEGRANATE (ABOUT ¼ CUP)

SHAVINGS OF PARMESAN CHEESE, FOR GARNISH (ABOUT ¼ CUP)

For the vinaigrette

1 SHALLOT, MINCED

3 TABLESPOONS BALSAMIC VINEGAR

¼ CUP EXTRA VIRGIN OLIVE OIL

1 TABLESPOON DIJON MUSTARD

1 TABLESPOON POMEGRANATE MOLASSES (OR HONEY)

KOSHER SALT AND FRESHLY GROUND BLACK PEPPER

FOR THE SALAD

Preheat the oven to 400°F.

Toss the pumpkin with the olive oil and season with salt and pepper. Arrange in a single layer on a baking sheet and roast for 45 minutes, until fork tender. Let cool completely.

FOR THE VINAIGRETTE

In a small bowl, whisk all the ingredients together until emulsified.

Place the arugula in a large salad bowl. Top with roasted pumpkin, pepitas, and pomegranate seeds. Garnish with Parmesan shavings and serve with vinaigrette.

6 SERVINGS

PREP TIME: 25 MINUTES

INACTIVE PREP TIME: 20 MINUTES TO COOL PUMPKIN

COOK TIME: 45 MINUTES

dijon brussels sprouts

Brussels sprouts taste so good with Dijon and a little lemon juice, they could convince even the pickiest eaters to "finish their vegetables." The bread crumbs add a nice texture and the dish perfectly complements the chicken with mushrooms and garlic (page 25).

Heat the olive oil in a large skillet over medium heat. Add the shallots and cook until translucent, about 4 minutes. Stir in Brussels sprouts and sauté until they begin to brown, 3 to 4 minutes. Add the chicken broth, lemon juice, mustard, and salt and pepper. Toss until mixed. Reduce the heat to low, cover, and simmer until sprouts are tender, 7 to 8 minutes. Remove the cover and increase heat to evaporate any excess liquid. Transfer to a serving platter and sprinkle with toasted bread crumbs.

6 SERVINGS
PREP TIME: 15 MINUTES
COOK TIME: 20 MINUTES

2 TABLESPOONS OLIVE OIL

2 SHALLOTS, THINLY SLICED

1½ POUNDS BRUSSELS SPROUTS, TRIMMED AND QUARTERED

½ CUP LOW-SODIUM CHICKEN BROTH

1½ TABLESPOONS FRESH LEMON JUICE

2 TABLESPOONS WHOLEGRAIN DIJON MUSTARD

KOSHER SALT AND FRESHLY GROUND BLACK PEPPER

¼ CUP FRESH BREAD CRUMBS, TOASTED

chicken with mushrooms and garlic

If I close my eyes while eating this dish, I'd swear I was in a little bistro in Provence. The flavors are so rich, and the chicken so tender it practically falls off the bone. I use thigh meat because it has more flavor and it's also less expensive, but if you prefer white meat, just substitute split breasts. Use the extra gravy on a side of mashed potatoes (see page 68) or simple brown rice.

Season the chicken with 1 tablespoon salt and 1 teaspoon pepper. Place 1 cup flour in a large dish. Dredge all the chicken thighs until coated in flour. Set aside in a single layer.

Heat a large Dutch oven over medium-high heat. Add the oil. Sear the chicken in batches, skin side down, for 4 to 5 minutes, until evenly browned. Do not turn the chicken or move it while it is browning, to encourage a good, golden crust on the skin. Remove the chicken to a plate and reserve.

Reduce the heat to medium and melt butter. Add the garlic and mushrooms. Cook until the garlic is golden brown and any liquid from the mushrooms has evaporated, 7 to 8 minutes. Add the rosemary and thyme and cook an additional 2 minutes. Stir in the white wine and chicken stock. Return the chicken to the Dutch oven. It is fine if the chicken is overlapping or in two layers. Bring the liquid to a low boil, then reduce to a gentle simmer. Cover and let cook 20 minutes. Remove the chicken to a platter and tent

continued

12 BONE-IN, SKIN-ON CHICKEN THIGHS

1 TABLESPOON PLUS 1 TEASPOON KOSHER SALT

1½ TEASPOONS FRESHLY GROUND BLACK PEPPER

1 CUP PLUS 3 TABLESPOONS ALL-PURPOSE FLOUR

1 TABLESPOON OLIVE OIL

1 TABLESPOON UNSALTED BUTTER

1 HEAD GARLIC, CLOVES SEPARATED AND PEELED

10 OUNCES WHITE BUTTON MUSHROOMS, STEMMED AND QUARTERED

1 TABLESPOON MINCED FRESH ROSEMARY

1 TABLESPOON MINCED FRESH THYME

¾ CUP WHITE WINE

2 CUPS LOW-SODIUM CHICKEN STOCK

3 TABLESPOONS HEAVY CREAM

1½ TABLESPOONS FRESH LEMON JUICE

¼ CUP WATER

TIP

Celebrate the bounty of the season's harvest by decorating with vegetables instead of flowers.

with foil to keep warm. Stir in cream, lemon juice, and remaining salt and pepper into the juices in the pot. Whisk the remaining 3 tablespoons flour with the water and stir into broth. Return the liquid to a low boil and cook until thickened, about 5 minutes. Serve the chicken with the gravy.

6 SERVINGS
PREP TIME: 30 MINUTES
COOK TIME: 45 MINUTES

hard apple cider

With this hard apple cider simmering on the stove, expect people to swoon when they walk through the front door. Simply delicious and can be served hot or poured over crushed ice.

In a saucepan, combine the cider, sugar, cinnamon, star anise, orange peel, and ginger. Bring to a low boil, and reduce heat to a simmer. Cover and cook 10 minutes. Strain and stir in Calvados. Serve hot, or chill and serve over crushed ice. Garnish with apple slices.

6 SERVINGS (ABOUT 5 CUPS)
PREP TIME: 5 MINUTES
COOK TIME: 10 MINUTES

1 QUART APPLE CIDER

2 TABLESPOONS SUGAR

1 CINNAMON STICK

2 WHOLE STAR ANISE

1 PIECE ORANGE PEEL (ABOUT 1 BY 4 INCHES)

$\frac{1}{2}$-INCH PIECE FRESH GINGER

$\frac{3}{4}$ CUP CALVADOS

THINLY SLICED APPLES, FOR GARNISH

rustic apple pie

This is a free-form apple pie, also known as a *crostata* in Italy. I like it when food doesn't look too perfect—think "rustic elegance." If I had to assign fall a flavor, it'd be this pie.

5 MEDIUM APPLES, PEELED, CORED, AND SLICED $\frac{1}{8}$-INCH THICK (ABOUT 4 CUPS)

$\frac{1}{3}$ CUP PLUS 3 TABLESPOONS LIGHTLY PACKED DARK BROWN SUGAR

2 TABLESPOONS CORNSTARCH

1 TABLESPOON FRESH LEMON JUICE

2 TEASPOONS GROUND CINNAMON

$\frac{1}{4}$ CUP OLD-FASHIONED ROLLED OATS

2 TABLESPOONS ALL-PURPOSE FLOUR

$\frac{1}{4}$ TEASPOON KOSHER SALT

3 TABLESPOONS UNSALTED BUTTER, MELTED

1 PIE CRUST FOR A 9-INCH PIE, HOMEMADE OR STORE-BOUGHT (ROLLED TO AN 11- TO 12-INCH DIAMETER)

1 EGG, LIGHTLY BEATEN

1 TABLESPOON RAW SUGAR

Preheat the oven to 400°F. Line a baking sheet with parchment paper.

In a large bowl, combine the apples with ⅓ cup brown sugar, the cornstarch, lemon juice, and cinnamon. In another small bowl, combine the remaining 3 tablespoons brown sugar, the oats, flour, salt, and butter.

Place pie crust on the prepared baking sheet. Spoon the apple mixture in the middle of the pie, leaving about a 1½-inch border. Fold crust edges over the filling, pleating occasionally. Spoon oat mixture over apples. Brush the crust with the egg and sprinkle with the raw sugar. Bake 40 to 45 minutes until crust is golden brown and apples are tender.

6 TO 8 SERVINGS
PREP TIME: 20 MINUTES
COOK TIME: 45 MINUTES

steakhouse night at home

Every Friday night, we would go to my grandparents' house for dinner. My grandpa would light the grill and he'd cook up some steaks. Dinner was always the same: steak, baked potatoes, and cream peas (I wasn't big on the peas so now I make creamed spinach). Since I was a kid, I only got a hamburger patty served with steak sauce. The pricier cuts of meat were reserved for the adults. We'd eat dinner and then watch the lottery winners and *Hee Haw*, and then my grandma, mom, and I would watch *Dallas* (which I probably had no business watching at that age, but I didn't know what was going on anyway).

I really love steakhouse-style food, but going to a steakhouse is ridiculously expensive. For about the cost of one person to dine out, you can make this entire meal at home. Family and guests are guaranteed to love this menu and it's a cinch to pull together.

MENU

SHRIMP COCKTAIL

ICEBERG WEDGE WITH BACON
AND BLUE CHEESE DRESSING

PORTERHOUSE STEAKS

BAKED POTATOES

CREAMED SPINACH

CHEESECAKE WITH CHERRY SAUCE

DIRTY MARTINI

SERVES 8

WINE

Cabernet Sauvignon

PLAYLIST

"Monterey" • BY FRANK SINATRA
"Everybody Loves Somebody Sometimes"
BY DEAN MARTIN
"Lady Is a Tramp" • BY FRANK SINATRA
"In the Mood" • BY GLENN MILLER
"Beyond the Sea" • BY BOBBY DARIN

shrimp cocktail

I love a good shrimp cocktail. When I was a kid and I'd see the grown-ups eating shrimp cocktail, I thought it looked so adult. Even though it's a really simple appetizer, there's something about it that just says "special."

Bring a large pot of water to a boil over high heat. Add the Old Bay and lemon juice. Add the shrimp and cook, uncovered, just until pink, about 2 minutes. Remove the shrimp and immediately place in a bowl of ice water until cool, about 2 minutes. Drain well.

In a small bowl, stir together the ketchup, horseradish, Worcestershire, and hot sauce (if using).

To serve, place the sauce in a bowl and arrange shrimp and lemon wedges alongside.

8 SERVINGS
PREP TIME: 20 MINUTES
COOK TIME: 3 MINUTES

1 TABLESPOON OLD BAY SEASONING

JUICE OF 1 LEMON

16 LARGE SHRIMP, PEELED AND DEVEINED

1 CUP KETCHUP

2 TABLESPOONS CREAMED HORSE-RADISH SAUCE

$\frac{1}{4}$ TEASPOON WORCESTERSHIRE SAUCE

HOT SAUCE (OPTIONAL)

LEMON WEDGES, FOR GARNISH

iceberg wedge with bacon and blue cheese dressing

Oh yeah ... bring on the iceberg wedge. I don't care that iceberg lettuce doesn't have as much nutritional value as other leafy greens—it's still my favorite part of a steakhouse dinner. It's so crunchy and crisp, and pairs perfectly with smoky bacon and creamy blue cheese dressing.

8 SLICES THICK-CUT BACON, DICED

$\frac{1}{2}$ CUP MAYONNAISE

$\frac{1}{2}$ CUP SOUR CREAM

1 TABLESPOON FRESH LEMON JUICE

$\frac{1}{4}$ TEASPOON KOSHER SALT

$\frac{1}{4}$ TEASPOON FRESHLY GROUND BLACK PEPPER

$\frac{1}{2}$ CUP CRUMBLED BLUE CHEESE

2 HEADS ICEBERG LETTUCE, OUTER LEAVES REMOVED, CUT INTO QUARTERS

1 CUP GRAPE OR CHERRY TOMATOES, CUT IN HALF

2 TABLESPOONS MINCED FRESH CHIVES

Cook the bacon in a skillet over medium heat until crispy. Drain on paper towels.

In a bowl, stir together the mayonnaise, sour cream, lemon juice, salt, and pepper until well blended. Stir in the blue cheese.

Arrange the iceberg wedges on a platter and scatter around the tomatoes. Spoon the blue cheese dressing over the lettuce. Top with bacon and chives.

8 SERVINGS
PREP TIME: 15 MINUTES
COOK TIME: 8 MINUTES

steakhouse night at home

porterhouse steaks

The mere thought of these steaks makes my mouth water. And they are super simple to prepare—you only need four ingredients. Buy good-quality meat and there's no need to dress it up with anything. My dogs get so excited when we have porterhouse steaks because they know there's a bone coming their way.

Preheat a gas or charcoal grill or place a grill pan over medium-high heat.

Combine the salt and pepper and sprinkle on both sides of each steak. Drizzle each side of steaks with canola oil.

Grill for 4 to 6 minutes on each side for medium-rare. Let the steaks rest a few minutes before slicing and serving.

4 PORTERHOUSE STEAKS

2 TABLESPOONS KOSHER SALT

2 TEASPOONS FRESHLY GROUND
  BLACK PEPPER

4 TABLESPOONS CANOLA OIL

8 SERVINGS
PREP TIME: 20 MINUTES
INACTIVE PREP TIME: 5 MINUTES
COOK TIME: 10 TO 12 MINUTES

TIP

Get to know your butcher.
He can guide you to the
best available cuts of meat.

baked potatoes

A good old-fashioned baked potato is worth its weight in gold, in my opinion. I eat mine almost ritualistically. First: butter, sour cream, salt, and pepper. Then, when I get to the skins—my favorite part—I spread them with a thick layer of butter and more salt and pepper.

8 BAKING POTATOES

1 TABLESPOON CANOLA OIL

2 TEASPOONS COARSE SEA SALT

TOPPINGS: BUTTER, SOUR CREAM,
  CHOPPED CHIVES, CRUMBLED
  COOKED BACON, GRATED CHEESE

Preheat the oven to 400°F. Use a fork to poke holes in each potato. Brush each potato with oil and sprinkle with salt. Place directly on oven rack and bake for about 1 hour, or until tender. Serve with a choice of toppings.

8 SERVINGS
PREP TIME: 5 MINUTES
COOK TIME: 60 MINUTES

creamed spinach

Creamed spinach is a great way to make a really healthy food taste good! A little butter and cream never hurt anybody, right? If you have any leftovers, make an omelet the next day and fill it with creamed spinach and cheese.

In a large skillet, melt the butter. Add the shallot and cook until translucent, 3 to 4 minutes. Add the spinach and lemon juice. Cover and let steam for 3 to 4 minutes. Remove the cover and use tongs to toss the spinach until all of it is wilted. Place the spinach in a colander and let any liquid drain.

Meanwhile, in the same skillet, heat the cream and nutmeg until the cream has thickened and reduced a bit, about 5 minutes. Stir in the Parmesan until melted. Add the spinach, salt, and pepper. Cook until heated through, 3 to 4 minutes.

8 SERVINGS
PREP TIME: 5 MINUTES
COOK TIME: 18 MINUTES

2 TABLESPOONS ($1/4$ STICK) UNSALTED BUTTER

1 SHALLOT, MINCED

2 POUNDS BABY SPINACH

1 TABLESPOON FRESH LEMON JUICE

1 CUP HEAVY CREAM

$1/2$ TEASPOON GROUND NUTMEG

$1/4$ CUP GRATED PARMESAN CHEESE

$1/2$ TEASPOON KOSHER SALT

$1/2$ TEASPOON FRESHLY GROUND BLACK PEPPER

cheesecake with cherry sauce

I can't eat a steak dinner without a piece of cheesecake for dessert. This recipe is New York–style, so it's more rich and creamy and a little more dense than regular cheesecake. While it is not a difficult dessert to prepare at all, the most common problem is that the top cracks. If this happens to you, no worries; just pour the cherry sauce all over the top and no one will be the wiser!

FOR THE CRUST

Preheat the oven to 350°F. In a medium bowl, combine the graham cracker crumbs and sugar. Stir in the butter. Transfer to a 9-inch springform pan. Use your fingers or a measuring cup to evenly press the crumb mixture onto the bottom of the pan and about 1 inch up the sides. Bake for 10 to 12 minutes, until golden brown. Cool completely on a wire rack.

Reduce oven temperature to 325°F.

FOR THE CHEESECAKE

Using an electric mixer on medium speed, beat the cream cheese until smooth and fluffy. Add the sugar and continue to mix. Add the eggs one at a time, beating well after each addition. Stir in the sour cream. Use the back of a knife to scrape out the vanilla seeds. Stir into cream cheese mixture.

Pour the batter into cooled crust and bake for 45 to 60 minutes, until lightly

For the crust
- 1½ CUPS GRAHAM CRACKER CRUMBS
- ¼ CUP SUGAR
- 6 TABLESPOONS (¾ STICK) UNSALTED BUTTER, MELTED

For the cheesecake
- TWO 8-OUNCE PACKAGES CREAM CHEESE, AT ROOM TEMPERATURE
- 1 CUP SUGAR
- 5 EXTRA LARGE EGGS, AT ROOM TEMPERATURE
- 1 CUP SOUR CREAM
- ½ VANILLA BEAN POD (SPLIT LENGTHWISE)

For the cherry sauce
- 2½ CUPS FROZEN CHERRIES (OR FRESH, PITTED)
- ¾ CUP SUGAR
- 2 TABLESPOONS FRESH LEMON JUICE
- 2 TABLESPOONS CORNSTARCH

continued

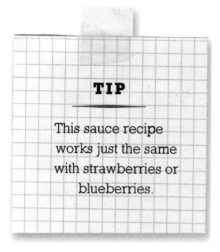

TIP

This sauce recipe works just the same with strawberries or blueberries.

browned on top. The center should still jiggle a little. Cool completely on a wire rack. Cover with plastic wrap and refrigerate at least 4 hours, until ready to serve.

FOR THE CHERRY SAUCE

While the cheesecake is cooling, in a small saucepan over medium-low heat, combine the cherries and sugar. Cook, stirring frequently. Combine the lemon juice and cornstarch until the starch dissolves and stir into the cherry mixture. Bring to a low boil. Reduce the heat to a simmer and stir until sauce thickens. Remove from the heat and let cool.

Serve the cheesecake with the cherry sauce.

8 SERVINGS
PREP TIME: 20 MINUTES
INACTIVE PREP TIME: 1½ HOURS FOR
    COOLING
COOK TIME: 60 MINUTES

dirty martini

Bond. James Bond. I always feel like saying that when I order a Martini. I'm an olive fanatic so I like my Martinis on the dirty side. If you like yours cleaner, just leave out the olive brine.

Combine the gin, olive brine, and vermouth in a cocktail shaker filled with ice. Shake vigorously. Strain into a martini glass and garnish with an olive.

2 OUNCES GIN

1 OUNCE OLIVE BRINE

SPLASH OF VERMOUTH

OLIVE

1 COCKTAIL
PREP TIME: 2 MINUTES

retro cocktail party

I am a TV junkie—a couch potato, if you will. There, I said it. I admit it. I even embrace it. Most of the stuff I enjoy watching is pretty mindless, with the exception of my favorite show, *Mad Men,* the story of a Madison Avenue advertising agency set in the early 1960s. I am totally mesmerized by each episode, not just because of the dark and twisted plots and spot-on acting (and handsome Jon Hamm doesn't hurt, either), but just as much by the costumes and prop styling and set design. It's obvious that no detail goes unnoticed.

Every time I tune in to *Mad Men,* I find myself wanting an old-fashioned cocktail. The show inspired me to make some retro appetizers and cocktails and this party was born. My friends and I had so much fun and it was a welcome change from the usual cocktail party.

MENU

MEATLOAF SLIDERS

SAUSAGE BALLS

OVEN-FRIED CHICKEN SATAY

ASPARAGUS WITH ROASTED GARLIC AÏOLI

DEVILS ON HORSEBACK

THE "PERFECT" MANHATTAN
WITH DRUNKEN CHERRIES

SERVES 12

PLAYLIST

"Tears Dry on Their Own" • BY AMY WINEHOUSE
"Mercy" • BY DUFFY
"Valerie" • BY MARK RONSON
"Come to Me" • BY KOOP
"Let's Get it On" • BY MARVIN GAYE
(DA PRODUCERS MPG GROOVE MIX)

WINE

This is a cocktail party—
I say spirits only, but
have a few bottles of
Cava on hand, just
in case!

meatloaf sliders

The most popular recipe from my first cookbook was meatloaf. I called it "manloaf" because if you make it for a man, he's destined to fall in love with you. Everyone loved it, even Oprah! So many people are serving sliders at parties that I decided to miniaturize my meatloaf for a party and turn it into a small sandwich—a meatloaf slider. These mini manloaves were the hit of the party!

Preheat the oven to 350°F. Line a baking sheet with parchment paper and place a cooling rack on top. Spray lightly with nonstick cooking spray.

In a large bowl, combine the beef, egg, ¼ cup of the ketchup, the onion, bread crumbs, Worcestershire, parsley, thyme, salt, pepper, and garlic powder. Use your hands to mix everything together.

Divide meat by the tablespoonful and shape each into a thin patty. Place on the prepared rack. Brush the patties with the remaining ¼ cup ketchup. Bake for 20 minutes.

While meatloaf is baking, spread mayonnaise onto one side of each bun. Place each meatloaf slider in a prepared bun and serve.

1 POUND EXTRA LEAN GROUND BEEF

1 LARGE EGG, LIGHTLY BEATEN

½ CUP KETCHUP

¼ CUP GRATED ONION

¼ CUP BREAD CRUMBS

1½ TEASPOONS WORCESTERSHIRE SAUCE

1 TABLESPOON MINCED FLAT-LEAF PARSLEY

1 TEASPOON MINCED FRESH THYME LEAVES

½ TEASPOON KOSHER SALT

½ TEASPOON FRESHLY GROUND BLACK PEPPER

¼ TEASPOON GARLIC POWDER

24 SLIDER-SIZE HAMBURGER BUNS

MAYONNAISE

12 SERVINGS (24 SLIDERS)

PREP TIME: 25 MINUTES

COOK TIME: 20 MINUTES

retro cocktail party

sausage balls

These are such a great cocktail party snack. They are so easy to eat and taste great. I also like to make these as an hors d'oeuvre at brunch parties. It is important to use freshly shredded cheese as it gives the dough more moisture.

1 POUND HOT ITALIAN SAUSAGE, CASINGS REMOVED

2½ CUPS BAKING MIX (I USE BISQUICK)

3 CUPS FRESHLY SHREDDED SHARP CHEDDAR CHEESE

¼ CUP HEAVY CREAM

12 SERVINGS
(ABOUT 50 BALLS)
PREP TIME: 15 MINUTES
COOK TIME: 15 MINUTES

Preheat the oven to 400°F. Line a baking sheet with parchment paper.

In a large bowl, combine the sausage meat, baking mix, and cheese. Use your hands to completely mix until well blended. The dough will be crumbly. Use your hands to roll into 1½-inch balls and place on the prepared baking sheet. Brush each sausage ball with heavy cream. Bake until golden brown, about 15 minutes.

oven-fried chicken satay

I love to serve fried food at parties, but when there's a big crowd, I find myself stuck in the kitchen frying while all of my guests are having fun. By coating chicken in cornflakes and baking it, I get the same crunchy effect without all of the labor. I like to serve this with my homemade BBQ sauce (see BBQ Chicken, page 245), but you could also use honey mustard, ranch dressing, or duck sauce.

Preheat the oven to 400°F. Line a baking sheet with parchment paper and spray with non-stick cooking spray.

Thread chicken pieces onto skewers, working the skewer in and out of the meat. Using a pastry brush, brush each piece of chicken with Dijon mustard.

In a food processor, combine the cornflakes, sage, thyme, salt, and pepper. Pulse to a coarse meal and transfer to a shallow dish. Dredge each chicken skewer in the cornflake mixture until evenly coated. Place on prepared baking sheet and bake until cooked through, 8 to 10 minutes.

Serve with BBQ sauce.

12 SERVINGS (ABOUT 28 SKEWERS)
PREP TIME: 25 MINUTES
COOK TIME: 8 MINUTES

1½ POUNDS BONELESS, SKINLESS CHICKEN BREASTS, CUT INTO STRIPS

⅓ CUP DIJON MUSTARD

4 CUPS CORNFLAKES

2 TEASPOONS MINCED FRESH SAGE

2 TEASPOONS MINCED FRESH THYME

¾ TEASPOON KOSHER SALT

¼ TEASPOON FRESHLY GROUND BLACK PEPPER

BBQ SAUCE, FOR SERVING

SPECIAL EQUIPMENT: SKEWERS

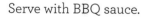

49

asparagus with roasted garlic aïoli

This is a great hors d'oeuvre to make ahead of time for a cocktail party. I steam the asparagus and make the aïoli the day before and store them in the refrigerator until serving time.

1 BUNCH ASPARAGUS, TRIMMED
    AND PEELED

1 HEAD OF GARLIC

1 TEASPOON OLIVE OIL

1 CUP MAYONNAISE

1 TABLESPOON FRESH LEMON JUICE

Bring a large pot of salted water to a boil. Prepare an ice water bath. Boil the asparagus for 2 minutes and plunge into the ice water. Drain and chill until serving time.

Preheat the oven to 400°F. Slice the top off the head of garlic. Place the garlic on a sheet of aluminum foil and drizzle with the olive oil. Wrap tightly. Roast for 35 to 50 minutes, depending on the size of the garlic, until the garlic is soft and deep golden brown. Let cool completely. Squeeze the peel of each clove to release the garlic.

In a food processor, combine the roasted garlic, mayonnaise, and lemon juice. Pulse until garlic is completely incorporated. Serve alongside the chilled asparagus.

12 SERVINGS
PREP TIME: 10 MINUTES
INACTIVE PREP TIME: 30 MINUTES (TO COOL
    GARLIC)
COOK TIME: 45 MINUTES

TIP

Save the leftover aïoli for sandwiches.

devils on horseback

People go crazy for these bite-size snacks, which only take minutes to prepare. This is an easy recipe to experiment with—you can substitute almonds for the pecans, prunes for the dates, or prosciutto for the bacon.

24 PECAN HALVES

24 PITTED DATES

8 SLICES BACON (NOT THICK-CUT), CUT CROSSWISE INTO THIRDS

1½ TO 2 CUPS MANGO CHUTNEY

Preheat the oven to 400°F. Line a baking sheet with parchment paper.

Insert a pecan half into each date. Wrap with a piece of bacon and secure with a toothpick. Place on prepared baking sheet. Bake until bacon is crisp, 8 to 10 minutes. Drain on a paper towel and serve with mango chutney for dipping.

12 SERVINGS (24 PIECES)
PREP TIME: 15 MINUTES
COOK TIME: 8 MINUTES

the "perfect" manhattan with drunken cherries

For this recipe, I turned to my two favorite cocktail guru girls, Leanne Shear and Tracey Toomey. The duo has their own Hamptons-based TV show and penned the novel *The Perfect Manhattan* and the drink guide *Cocktail Therapy*.

2 OUNCES BOURBON

½ OUNCE GOOD-QUALITY SWEET
    VERMOUTH

DASH OF BITTERS

1 DRUNKEN CHERRY (RECIPE FOL-
    LOWS)

In a cocktail shaker filled with ice, combine the bourbon, vermouth, and bitters. Shake for 15 seconds. Strain into a chilled martini glass and garnish with the Drunken Cherry.

1 COCKTAIL
PREP TIME: 2 MINUTES

drunken cherries

Fill a 1-quart mason jar with fresh, plump cherries (pits removed). Pour your favorite bourbon over them until they are all covered. Seal the jar and refrigerate at least 24 hours, but the cherries will keep for up to 3 months. The longer they marinate in the bourbon, the better they taste! These cherries are great in Manhattans, Old Fashioneds, or even over vanilla ice cream for a decadent dessert.

1 QUART CHERRIES
PREP TIME: 3 MINUTES
INACTIVE PREP TIME: 24 HOURS OR MORE

thanksgiving

What could be better than a holiday devoted to eating? No pressure to buy gifts—just cooking, eating, drinking, and enjoying each other's company. Honestly, nothing is better in my book. I look forward to Thanksgiving all year long.

I like to serve Thanksgiving in the afternoon. We start with cocktails and light hors d'oeuvres and then dive into the main event. I decorate in autumnal colors with flowers and gourds, elegant but nothing too fancy. Everyone fills up, hits the couch, and then goes for round two in the evening.

MENU

WILD MUSHROOM–PARMESAN GRITS CAKES

SPICED PEPITAS AND PECANS

HERB-ROASTED MAPLE-ORANGE GLAZED
TURKEY WITH SPICY CORNBREAD STUFFING
AND GIBLET GRAVY

CARAMELIZED SHALLOT MASHED
RED-SKINNED POTATOES

SWEET POTATO CASSEROLE
(from Sunday Supper, on page 86)

CRISP GREEN BEANS
WITH SUN-DRIED TOMATOES

APPLE-ORANGE-CRANBERRY RELISH

SAGE BUTTERMILK BISCUITS

GINGER ROYALE

PUMPKIN ROLL

SERVES 8

WINE

Beaujolais Nouveau
Pinot Noir
Sangiovese

PLAYLIST

"Diamonds on the Inside" • BY BEN HARPER
"With a Little Help from my Friends" • BY JOE COCKER
"1963" • BY RACHEL YAMAGATA
"Babylon 2" • BY DAVID GRAY
"The Show" • BY LENKA

wild mushroom–parmesan grits cakes

I make grits cakes for parties all the time. Anything can be added to the grits—sometimes I mix in chorizo or rock shrimp, Cheddar or Asiago—and they are always a success. For Thanksgiving, I like using mushrooms and Parmesan for a nice, rich flavor. Since it's a holiday, I like to make the grits cakes extra special by adding mushroom ragout.

FOR THE GRITS CAKES

Heat 1 tablespoon of the olive oil in a small skillet over medium heat. Add the mushrooms and cook about 5 minutes, until all of the liquid is released and they are golden brown. Season with salt and pepper. Set aside.

In a large saucepan over medium-high heat, combine the chicken stock, milk, and 1 teaspoon salt, and bring to a gentle boil. Stir in the saffron threads until dissolved, about 2 minutes. Slowly whisk in the grits and reduce the heat to a very low simmer, stirring occasionally to keep the grits from scorching. Cook, stirring frequently until the liquid has been absorbed and the grits are thick, about 30 minutes. Stir in the reserved mushrooms, and the cheese, butter, and ½ teaspoon pepper.

Grease a 13 by 9-inch baking dish. Pour in the grits and smooth out into an even layer. Let cool completely. Cover with plastic wrap and refrigerate for 2 hours or up to overnight.

Use a 2½-inch biscuit cutter to cut out 15 cakes. Place on a baking sheet in one layer, cover, and refrigerate until ready to cook.
continued

For the grits cakes

4 TABLESPOONS OLIVE OIL

½ CUP FINELY DICED WHITE BUTTON MUSHROOMS

KOSHER SALT AND FRESHLY GROUND BLACK PEPPER

3 CUPS LOW-SODIUM CHICKEN STOCK

3 CUPS REDUCED-FAT MILK

1 TEASPOON KOSHER SALT

⅛ TEASPOON SAFFRON THREADS

2 CUPS REGULAR GRITS (NOT INSTANT OR QUICK-COOKING)

½ CUP GRATED PARMESAN CHEESE

1 TABLESPOON UNSALTED BUTTER

½ TEASPOON FRESHLY GROUND BLACK PEPPER

SPECIAL EQUIPMENT: 2½-INCH BISCUIT CUTTER

For the mushroom ragout

2 TABLESPOONS ($\frac{1}{4}$ STICK) UNSALTED BUTTER

1 GARLIC CLOVE, MINCED

1 SPRIG FRESH ROSEMARY

2 CUPS MIXED WILD MUSHROOMS (SUCH AS CHANTERELLE, PORCINI, OYSTER, OR SHIITAKE)

1 TABLESPOON FRESH LEMON JUICE

$\frac{1}{4}$ TEASPOON KOSHER SALT

$\frac{1}{4}$ TEASPOON FRESHLY GROUND BLACK PEPPER

1 TABLESPOON HEAVY CREAM

FOR THE MUSHROOM RAGOUT

Melt the butter with garlic and rosemary in a medium skillet over medium heat. Add mushrooms and cook for 8 to 10 minutes, until all of the liquid is released and the mushrooms are golden brown. Season with the salt and pepper and stir in lemon juice and heavy cream. Cook about 2 more minutes, until cream is absorbed. Remove rosemary.

TO FINISH

Use the remaining olive oil to grease a nonstick griddle over medium heat. Gently blot the grits cakes with paper towels to make sure they are not damp. Cook the cakes 4 to 5 minutes on each side, until golden brown. Garnish with the mushroom ragout.

15 SERVINGS
PREP TIME: 10 MINUTES
INACTIVE PREP TIME: 2 HOURS UP TO OVERNIGHT
COOK TIME: 1 HOUR

spiced pepitas and pecans

These are a delicious homemade version of "bar nuts." I use pepitas as a nod to the season and pecans for my Southern heritage, but any combination of nuts works.

Preheat the oven to 300°F. Line a baking sheet with parchment paper.

In a small bowl, combine sugar, cinnamon, allspice, cumin, salt, and cayenne. Set aside. In a large bowl, beat the egg whites and water until frothy. Stir in the pepitas and pecans, then add sugar mixture. Toss until nuts are completely coated.

Evenly spread nuts on the prepared baking sheet. Bake 20 to 25 minutes, until crispy. Let cool completely. Store in an airtight container.

4 CUPS
PREP TIME: 7 MINUTES
INACTIVE PREP TIME: 30 MINUTES TO COOL
COOK TIME: 25 TO 30 MINUTES

$\frac{1}{2}$ CUP LIGHTLY PACKED LIGHT BROWN SUGAR

$1\frac{1}{2}$ TEASPOONS GROUND CINNAMON

$\frac{1}{2}$ TEASPOON GROUND ALLSPICE

$\frac{1}{2}$ TEASPOON GROUND CUMIN

$\frac{1}{2}$ TEASPOON KOSHER SALT

PINCH OF CAYENNE PEPPER

2 LARGE EGG WHITES

1 TABLESPOON WATER

2 CUPS RAW PEPITAS (SHELLED PUMPKIN SEEDS)

2 CUPS SHELLED PECAN HALVES

TIP

Make extra to keep on hand throughout the holiday season. Perfect for a snack for drop-in guests or a last-minute gift.

herb-roasted maple-orange glazed turkey with spicy cornbread stuffing and giblet gravy

I don't like to brag, but I really do make an excellent turkey! Herb butter under the skin flavors the bird, and basting with maple syrup and orange juice makes the skin beautifully golden brown—it looks like it's straight out of a magazine every time. The giblet gravy mellows the subtle heat of the cornbread stuffing and pulls it all together.

FOR THE STUFFING

Make the Herb Butter, below, and Spicy Cornbread, see page 67.

In a medium skillet over medium heat, melt the herb butter. Add the onions and celery and sauté until translucent, stirring occasionally, 10 to 15 minutes. Remove from heat and let cool completely.

In a large bowl, combine onions and celery with the cornbread, egg, milk, chicken broth, salt, and pepper. Mix well to combine. Refrigerate until time to stuff the turkey.

FOR THE HERB BUTTER

In a small mixing bowl, combine the butter with the herbs, salt, and pepper. Set aside.

For the stuffing

¼ CUP SOFTENED HERB BUTTER (RECIPE FOLLOWS)

6 CUPS CUBED SPICY CORNBREAD (RECIPE FOLLOWS)

2 YELLOW ONIONS, FINELY DICED

2 CELERY STALKS, FINELY DICED

1 LARGE EGG, LIGHTLY BEATEN

½ CUP MILK

¾ CUP LOW-SODIUM CHICKEN BROTH

½ TEASPOON KOSHER SALT

½ TEASPOON FRESHLY GROUND BLACK PEPPER

For the herb butter

1 CUP (2 STICKS) UNSALTED BUTTER, SOFTENED

3 TABLESPOONS MINCED FRESH SAGE

2 TABLESPOONS MINCED FRESH THYME

2 TABLESPOONS MINCED FRESH FLAT-LEAF PARSLEY

1 TEASPOON MINCED FRESH ROSEMARY

2 TABLESPOONS KOSHER SALT

2 TEASPOONS FRESHLY GROUND BLACK PEPPER

continued

FOR THE TURKEY

Preheat the oven to 350°F. Grease a baking dish.

Remove neck, giblets, and gizzards from the cavity and reserve for the gravy. Liberally season turkey all over with salt and pepper, including inside the cavity. Using your fingers, gently lift the skin and rub the remaining herb butter all over the bird under the skin. Stuff the turkey with about one-third of the cornbread stuffing (be sure not to pack in too tightly), and bake the remaining in the prepared baking dish and cover with aluminum foil. Truss the turkey, place on a rack in a large roasting pan, and put into the oven.

In a small saucepan over low heat, combine the maple syrup, chicken broth, orange juice, and bay leaf. Let come to a very low simmer and remove from the heat. Baste the turkey every 30 minutes with this mixture.

When the turkey has cooked for about 2 hours, make the gravy.

FOR THE GRAVY

In a medium saucepan over medium-high heat, combine the giblets and neck (discard the liver and heart) with the stock, bouillon cube, and bay leaf. Bring to a boil, reduce the heat, cover, and sim-

For the turkey

ONE 12- TO 14-POUND FRESH
   TURKEY, RINSED AND PATTED DRY

KOSHER SALT AND FRESHLY
   GROUND BLACK PEPPER

¾ CUP SOFTENED HERB BUTTER

¾ CUP MAPLE SYRUP

¼ CUP CHICKEN BROTH

¼ CUP FRESH ORANGE JUICE

1 BAY LEAF

8 TO 10 SERVINGS
PREP TIME: 40 MINUTES
INACTIVE PREP TIME: 20 MINUTES
   (TO REST TURKEY)
COOK TIME: 3 TO 3½ HOURS

For the gravy

RESERVED TURKEY GIBLETS AND
   NECK

4 CUPS TURKEY STOCK OR
   CHICKEN STOCK

1 CHICKEN BOUILLON CUBE

1 BAY LEAF

¾ CUP WATER

3 TABLESPOONS ALL-PURPOSE
   FLOUR

KOSHER SALT AND FRESHLY
   GROUND BLACK PEPPER

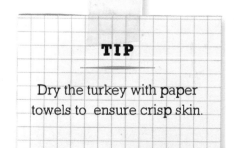

TIP

Dry the turkey with paper towels to ensure crisp skin.

mer for 30 minutes. Add ½ cup water and cook for 30 minutes more. Remove from the heat and strain. Return to the pan and bring to a boil.

In a small bowl, combine the flour and ¼ cup water. Whisk vigorously into boiling stock. Reduce heat to a simmer and cook an additional 3 to 4 minutes, stirring constantly, until mixture thickens. Season with salt and pepper to taste. Keep warm and serve with turkey.

The turkey will take about 3 to 3½ hours to cook, 15 to 20 minutes per pound. The turkey is done when a meat thermometer reaches 170°F in the meatiest part of the thigh and the juices run clear. If the breast or legs look as if they are cooking too rapidly, tent with foil. When the turkey is done, remove it from the oven, tent with foil, and let rest 20 minutes.

Transfer the turkey to a cutting board and carve. Serve with the stuffing and gravy.

spicy cornbread

Preheat the oven to 375°F. Grease a 13 by 9 by 2-inch baking dish and place in the oven to heat while you make the batter.

In a large bowl, combine the cornmeal, baking powder, sugar, red pepper flakes, and salt. Stir to combine. Add the milk, oil, and corn, and stir until just combined. Stir in the onion, green pepper, and cheese just until incorporated.

Carefully remove the hot baking dish from the oven and pour the batter into it. Return to the oven and bake for 35 to 40 minutes, or until a toothpick comes out clean. Let cool completely.

3 CUPS YELLOW CORNMEAL

2 TABLESPOONS BAKING POWDER

2 TABLESPOONS SUGAR

2 TEASPOONS RED PEPPER FLAKES

2½ TEASPOONS KOSHER SALT

2 CUPS MILK

½ CUP CANOLA OIL

ONE 14.75-OUNCE CAN CREAM-STYLE CORN

1 YELLOW ONION, FINELY DICED

½ CUP DICED GREEN BELL PEPPER

1 CUP GRATED SHARP CHEDDAR CHEESE

ONE 13 BY 9-INCH PAN
PREP TIME: 10 MINUTES
INACTIVE PREP TIME: 2 HOURS TO COOL
COOK TIME: 35 TO 40 MINUTES

caramelized shallot mashed red-skinned potatoes

I make mashed potatoes all the time, so for Thanksgiving I like to make them a little more special by stirring in caramelized shallots.

For the caramelized shallots

3 TABLESPOONS UNSALTED BUTTER

1 TABLESPOON OLIVE OIL

2 TABLESPOONS LIGHT BROWN SUGAR

10 SHALLOTS, THINLY SLICED

$\frac{1}{4}$ TEASPOON KOSHER SALT

$\frac{1}{4}$ TEASPOON FRESHLY GROUND BLACK PEPPER

For the potatoes

4 POUNDS UNPEELED RED POTATOES, SCRUBBED AND CUT INTO 1$\frac{1}{2}$-INCH CUBES

3 TEASPOONS KOSHER SALT

1 CUP WHOLE MILK

8 TABLESPOONS (1 STICK) UNSALTED BUTTER

1 TEASPOON FRESHLY GROUND BLACK PEPPER

8 TO 10 SERVINGS

PREP TIME: 25 MINUTES

COOK TIME: 1 HOUR AND 10 MINUTES FOR THE SHALLOTS, 40 MINUTES FOR THE POTATOES

FOR THE SHALLOTS

In a medium skillet over medium heat, melt the butter with the olive oil. Stir in the brown sugar until dissolved. Add the shallots and stir occasionally until they begin to brown, about 10 minutes. Stir in 1 tablespoon water, reduce the heat to low, and cover partially.

Cook about 1 hour, stirring every 20 minutes and adding an additional tablespoon of water if shallots are drying out or sticking. Stir in the salt and pepper.

Set aside until the mashed potatoes are ready. (The shallots can be made a few days ahead of time and stored in the refrigerator, then reheated at serving time.)

FOR THE POTATOES

Place the potatoes in a stockpot. Cover with cold water and add 1 teaspoon salt. Bring to a boil over medium-high heat. Lower the heat to a simmer and cool until the potatoes are fork tender, about 20 minutes. Drain and return the potatoes to the pan.

Meanwhile, in a small saucepan over medium heat, heat the milk and butter.

Use a potato masher to begin mashing potatoes. Slowly add in milk mixture and continue to mash. Potatoes should be smooth with some chunks. Stir in reserved shallots, 2 teaspoons salt, and 1 teaspoon pepper.

crisp green beans with sun-dried tomatoes

Thanksgiving dinner can be a little heavy, so I like to have a light side dish like these crisp green beans with sun-dried tomatoes. They add nice color to the buffet and are a healthy addition to the meal.

Prepare an ice water bath. Bring a large pot of salted water to a boil over high heat. Add the green beans and cook 2 minutes. Drain the beans and plunge into the ice water to stop the cooking. Drain. (This step can be done the day before. Refrigerate beans until ready to finish.)

In a large skillet, melt the butter over medium heat. Add the shallots and sauté until tender, about 3 minutes. Add the tomatoes and cook 2 minutes. Add the beans, lemon zest, salt, and pepper. Cook until the beans are heated through, about 5 minutes.

8 TO 10 SERVINGS
PREP TIME: 20 MINUTES
INACTIVE PREP TIME: 5 MINUTES TO
    COOL BEANS
COOK TIME: 12 MINUTES

3 POUNDS FRENCH GREEN BEANS, TRIMMED

3 TABLESPOONS UNSALTED BUTTER

2 SHALLOTS, MINCED

1 CUP DICED SUN-DRIED TOMATOES

1 TABLESPOON FRESHLY GRATED LEMON ZEST

$\frac{3}{4}$ TEASPOON KOSHER SALT

$\frac{1}{2}$ TEASPOON FRESHLY GROUND BLACK PEPPER

apple-orange-cranberry relish

I was always kind of lukewarm about cranberry relish until my
mom shared this recipe with me. Now, I can't get enough of it.
I eat seconds and thirds and make it all throughout the winter.
DELICIOUS!

1 ORANGE

3 CUPS FRESH CRANBERRIES

1 MEDIUM APPLE (A SWEETER
   VARIETY SUCH AS GALA OR FUJI)

1 CELERY STALK, CUT INTO 1-INCH
   PIECES

$\frac{1}{2}$ CUP SHELLED WALNUTS

$\frac{3}{4}$ CUP SUGAR

1 TABLESPOON ORANGE LIQUEUR

Grate the zest from the whole orange
and set aside. Cut off any remaining pith
from the orange. Cut the orange into
chunks.

In a food processor, combine cranberries,
orange chunks, orange zest, apple, and
celery and process until finely chopped.
Be careful not to process too long because mixture will become mushy. Add
the walnuts and pulse until chopped.
Stir in the sugar and orange liqueur.
Refrigerate until serving time.

3 CUPS
PREP TIME: 15 MINUTES

sage buttermilk biscuits

Biscuits were always a mainstay of my Southern childhood, and when I tried adding sage to my grandma's recipe, they became the perfect bread for Thanksgiving dinner. Any herb can be substituted, so experiment with your favorite.

2½ TO 3 CUPS ALL-PURPOSE FLOUR

8 TABLESPOONS (1 STICK) UNSALTED BUTTER, CHILLED AND CUT INTO CUBES

1 TABLESPOON BAKING POWDER

¼ TEASPOON BAKING SODA

1 TEASPOON KOSHER SALT

1 TEASPOON SUGAR

1 TABLESPOON MINCED FRESH SAGE

1 CUP BUTTERMILK

2 TABLESPOONS HEAVY CREAM

4 TABLESPOONS (½ STICK) UNSALTED BUTTER, SOFTENED

SPECIAL EQUIPMENT: PASTRY BLENDER AND 3-INCH BISCUIT CUTTER

20 TO 22 BISCUITS
PREP TIME: 20 MINUTES
COOK TIME: 12 MINUTES

Preheat oven to 450°F. Grease a baking sheet.

In a large mixing bowl, combine 2½ cups flour and the chilled butter. Using a pastry blender, cut the butter into the flour until it resembles a coarse meal. Stir in the baking powder, baking soda, salt, sugar, and sage. Make a well in the center and pour in the buttermilk. Mix with a fork until all of the ingredients are incorporated and the dough begins to shape into a ball. (The dough will be slightly dry.)

Sprinkle a work surface with flour, coat your palms, and rub some on a rolling pin. Turn out the dough onto the work surface. Knead the dough for 1 to 2 minutes, folding it over onto itself each time. Roll the dough to about ½-inch thick. Flour a 3-inch biscuit cutter (or the rim of a glass) and cut out the biscuits. Reshape the leftover dough into a ball, roll it out again, and cut out more biscuits until there is no dough remaining.

Place the biscuits on the baking sheet and brush with cream. Bake for 10 to 12 minutes, until the tops are golden brown. While the biscuits are still hot, spread some softened butter on top of each one and let it melt.

ginger royale

This Ginger Royale is a play on one of my favorite cocktails, the Kir Royale, which pairs Champagne with a touch of crème de cassis. I use ginger liqueur in place of cassis for true holiday flavor.

Pour ginger liqueur into a champagne glass. Top with Champagne.

1 COCKTAIL
PREP TIME: 2 MINUTES

1 OUNCE GINGER LIQUEUR (SUCH AS DOMAINE DE CANTON)

3 OUNCES CHAMPAGNE

pumpkin roll

When I was a kid, this was one of my favorite holiday recipes. The lightness of the pumpkin cake and the richness of the cream cheese filling is a divine combination. It kind of looks like a yule log, so it can double as a *buche de Noël*!

For the cake

⅔ CUP ALL-PURPOSE FLOUR

1 TEASPOON BAKING POWDER

2 TEASPOONS GROUND CINNAMON

1 TEASPOON GROUND GINGER

½ TEASPOON GROUND NUTMEG

½ TEASPOON KOSHER SALT

3 LARGE EGGS

1 CUP WHITE SUGAR

½ CUP PURE PUMPKIN PUREE

½ CUP CONFECTIONERS' SUGAR

For the filling

1 CUP CONFECTIONERS' SUGAR, PLUS EXTRA FOR DUSTING

TWO 3-OUNCE PACKAGES CREAM CHEESE, SOFTENED

4 TABLESPOONS (½ STICK) UNSALTED BUTTER, SOFTENED

½ TEASPOON VANILLA EXTRACT

FOR THE CAKE

Preheat the oven to 375°F. Line a jelly-roll pan with parchment paper. Lightly grease and flour the paper.

In a medium bowl, combine the flour, baking powder, cinnamon, ginger, nutmeg, and salt.

In a separate large bowl, beat eggs and white sugar until light and fluffy, about 5 minutes. Mix in the pumpkin until combined. Slowly add the dry ingredients to the pumpkin mixture. Pour the batter out onto the prepared jelly-roll pan. Drop the pan twice on counter to even out the batter and release any bubbles. Bake for 15 minutes.

Meanwhile, dust a dishtowel with confectioners' sugar. Immediately transfer the cake to the powdered dishtowel and gently roll from one short end to the other. Refrigerate on a pan or plate until completely cool, about 2 hours.

FOR THE FILLING

Combine the confectioners' sugar, cream cheese, butter, and vanilla. Beat until light and fluffy.

Unroll the cake and spread with the filling. Reroll cake and wrap with plastic wrap for 1 to 2 hours. Dust with confectioners' sugar before serving.

8 SERVINGS

PREP TIME: 25 MINUTES

INACTIVE PREP TIME: 2 HOURS TO COOL CAKE, 1 TO 2 HOURS TO SET

COOK TIME: 15 MINUTES

thanksgiving

Thanksgiving may be my favorite, but the following day is a close second. My friend Max is from New Orleans, and one year he taught me how to make his secret turkey gumbo. It is to die for. With the leftover sweet potato casserole, I make shortcakes topped with leftover cranberry sauce. Oh, yeah . . .

max's turkey gumbo

After a wonderful Thanksgiving in Napa Valley one year, the next day our friend Max Loubiere, who is from New Orleans, decided to treat us to his family's recipe for turkey gumbo. Now I make it every year and freeze any that's left over—it's that good.

1 TURKEY CARCASS

8 TABLESPOONS (1 STICK) UNSALTED BUTTER

1 CUP ALL-PURPOSE FLOUR

2 YELLOW ONIONS, DICED

2 CELERY STALKS, DICED

1 GREEN BELL PEPPER, DICED

10 CUPS WATER

2 CHICKEN BOUILLON CUBES

1 POUND SMOKED SAUSAGE (SUCH AS KIELBASA), SLICED $\frac{1}{4}$-INCH THICK

1 TABLESPOON CREOLE SEASONING

KOSHER SALT AND FRESHLY GROUND BLACK PEPPER

STEAMED RICE, FOR SERVING

Remove the turkey meat from the carcass, dice, and set aside.

In a large Dutch oven over medium heat, melt the butter. Add the flour and reduce heat to low. Cook, stirring constantly, until the mixture is chocolate brown, about 15 minutes. Do not let it burn. Stir in the onions, celery, and green pepper and cook an additional 5 minutes. Stir in the water and bouillon cubes. Place the turkey carcass in the water and bring to a boil. Reduce the heat to a simmer and simmer for 4 hours. Remove the carcass. Add the reserved turkey meat and the sausage. Stir in the Creole seasoning and season with salt and pepper. Simmer 1 hour more. Serve with steamed rice.

8 SERVINGS
PREP TIME: 15 MINUTES
COOK TIME: 5$\frac{1}{2}$ TO 6 HOURS

sweet potato–cranberry shortcakes

These are the perfect way to use up leftover sweet potatoes and cranberry relish! You can substitute canned pumpkin for the sweet potatoes.

Preheat oven to 450°F. Grease a baking sheet.

In a large mixing bowl, combine the flour and butter. Using a pastry blender, cut the butter into the flour until it resembles a coarse meal. Stir in the baking powder, baking soda, salt, sugar, and cinnamon. Stir in the sweet potatoes until just combined. Make a well in the center and pour in the milk. Mix until all ingredients are incorporated and the dough begins to shape into a ball.

Sprinkle a work surface with flour, coat your palms, and rub some on a rolling pin. Turn out the dough onto the work surface. Knead the dough for 1 to 2 minutes, folding it over onto itself each time. Roll the dough to about ½-inch thick. Flour a 3-inch biscuit cutter (or the rim of a glass) and cut out the biscuits. Reshape the leftover dough into a ball, roll it out again, and cut out more biscuits until there is no dough remaining.

Place the biscuits on the baking sheet and bake for 10 to 12 minutes, until the tops are golden brown. While the biscuits are still hot, spread softened butter on top of each one and let it melt.

Split each biscuit in half and fill with a few tablespoons of cranberry relish and whipped cream.

2½ CUPS ALL-PURPOSE FLOUR, PLUS EXTRA FOR ROLLING

8 TABLESPOONS (1 STICK) UNSALTED BUTTER, CHILLED AND CUT INTO CUBES

1 TABLESPOON BAKING POWDER

¼ TEASPOON BAKING SODA

1 TEASPOON SALT

2 TABLESPOONS SUGAR

1 TEASPOON GROUND CINNAMON

1 CUP SWEET POTATO CASSEROLE (PAGE 86), WITHOUT THE MARSH-MALLOW TOPPING

⅓ CUP MILK

LEFTOVER CRANBERRY RELISH, WHIPPED CREAM, FOR SERVING

SPECIAL EQUIPMENT: PASTRY BLENDER AND 3-INCH BISCUIT CUTTER

12 TO 15 BISCUITS
PREP TIME: 20 MINUTES
COOK TIME: 10 TO 12 MINUTES

sunday supper

Having a Sunday supper each week is a wonderful tradition. It's a time for everyone to get together without any pressure and just relax and enjoy each other's company. We would go to my grandma's on Sunday for supper around two or three in the afternoon. She was always cooking up something good, whether it be pot roast, baked steak and gravy, or chicken and dumplings. We'd stuff ourselves silly and then around eight o'clock that night we'd find ourselves feeling peckish and head into the refrigerator for a second piece of pie.

I've carried on the Sunday supper tradition, and my favorite thing to make is fried chicken. It makes sense to prepare it on a Sunday because it takes a few hours to marinate. Sundays are laid back, so there's no rush to get dinner on the table. There's even time to make a pie.

MENU

TOMATO, VIDALIA ONION,
AND CUCUMBER SALAD

FRIED CHICKEN

SWEET POTATO CASSEROLE

SIMMERED COLLARD GREENS

FROZEN SOUTHSIDERS

CHOCOLATE BANANA CREAM PIE

SERVES 4 TO 6

WINE

*Chardonnay
Rosé*

PLAYLIST

"By the Time I Get to Phoenix" • BY GLEN CAMPBELL
"Sweet Home Alabama" • BY LYNYRD SKYNYRD
"I Feel It All" • BY FEIST
"Big Yellow Taxi" • BY JONI MITCHELL
"Honky Tonky Women" • BY THE ROLLING STONES
"Son of a Preacher Man" • BY DUSTY SPRINGFIELD

tomato, vidalia onion, and cucumber salad

Almost every evening in the summer, my grandma would slice up some tomatoes, onions, and cucumbers for us to snack on before dinner. She'd just sprinkle them with a little salt and pepper. Her predinner "crudités" inspired this salad. I like to serve it piled on a platter, and use different colors of tomatoes.

Arrange the tomato slices on a platter. In a medium bowl, combine the onion, cucumber, and cherry tomatoes. In a small bowl, whisk together the oil, vinegar, salt, and pepper. Add to the salad and toss to combine. Spoon the salad onto the sliced tomatoes. Garnish with the scallions.

4 TO 6 SERVINGS
PREP TIME: 15 MINUTES

3 RIPE TOMATOES, SLICED

1 VIDALIA ONION, HALVED AND THINLY SLICED

1 ENGLISH CUCUMBER, PEELED AND THINLY SLICED

$\frac{1}{2}$ CUP CHERRY TOMATOES, SLICED IN HALF

$\frac{1}{4}$ CUP EXTRA VIRGIN OLIVE OIL

$\frac{1}{4}$ CUP WHITE WINE VINEGAR

$\frac{1}{2}$ TEASPOON KOSHER SALT

$\frac{1}{2}$ TEASPOON FRESHLY GROUND BLACK PEPPER

2 SCALLIONS, THINLY SLICED (GREEN AND WHITE PARTS)

fried chicken

People always ask me what my favorite thing to cook is, and I have to say that I enjoy nothing more than fryin' up some chicken. The only thing I enjoy more than cooking it is eating it! Paula Deen taught me to cover the chicken for part of its cooking time so that it steams and keeps the meat juicy. I transfer my chicken to the oven for the last 10 minutes of cooking, which I find makes the skin really crisp. It also makes it really easy to fry in batches and keep all of the chicken hot. Don't be afraid of the hot sauce in the recipe—the chicken will not be spicy.

1 FRYER CHICKEN, CUT INTO 10 PIECES

1 TABLESPOON KOSHER SALT

2 TEASPOONS FRESHLY GROUND BLACK PEPPER

1 TEASPOON GARLIC POWDER

3 LARGE EGGS

½ CUP HOT SAUCE

½ CUP BUTTERMILK

PEANUT OIL

2½ CUPS SELF-RISING FLOUR

Season the chicken on both sides with salt, pepper, and garlic powder. In a large bowl, big enough to accommodate all of the chicken, whisk the eggs, hot sauce, and buttermilk. Add the chicken and toss to combine. Cover and refrigerate. Let marinate at least 2 and up to 4 hours.

In a large Dutch oven, heat a couple inches of peanut oil to 350°F. Preheat oven to 450°F.

Dredge the chicken in the flour, taking care to evenly coat each piece. Transfer in batches to the hot oil. Cover and let cook 5 minutes. Remove the cover and turn the chicken. Let cook uncovered an additional 5 minutes. Place the chicken on a baking sheet and bake 10 minutes. Serve immediately.

4 TO 6 SERVINGS
PREP TIME: 10 MINUTES
INACTIVE PREP TIME: 2 TO 4 HOURS TO MARINATE CHICKEN
COOK TIME: 20 MINUTES

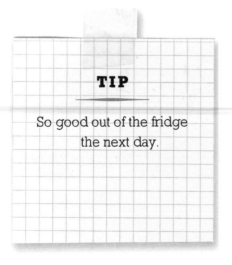

TIP

So good out of the fridge the next day.

sweet potato casserole

Sweet potatoes are yummy, and also a valuable food for boosting antioxidants in the body. For this recipe, I whip them with spices, put them in a baking dish, and cover them with marshmallows. The marshmallows get golden brown and crunchy and taste fantastic with the sweet potatoes. I could almost eat this for dessert!

4 LARGE SWEET POTATOES (ABOUT 4 POUNDS), PEELED AND CUT INTO CHUNKS

1 CUP MILK

½ CUP HEAVY CREAM

4 TABLESPOONS (½ STICK) UNSALTED BUTTER

2 TABLESPOONS LIGHT BROWN SUGAR

2 TEASPOONS KOSHER SALT

2 TEASPOONS GROUND CINNAMON

1 TEASPOON GROUND NUTMEG

1 TEASPOON GROUND GINGER

ONE 16-OUNCE BAG LARGE MARSHMALLOWS

Preheat the oven to 350°F. Grease a 4-quart baking dish.

Place the sweet potatoes in a medium pot. Cover with cold water. Bring to a boil over medium-high heat. Lower the heat to a simmer and cook until potatoes are fork tender, 20 to 25 minutes. Drain.

Meanwhile, in a small saucepan, heat the milk, cream, and butter until warm but not simmering.

Return the potatoes to the pot and add warm milk mixture, sugar, salt, cinnamon, nutmeg, and ginger. Using a handheld mixer, whip the potatoes until smooth and creamy with no lumps. Transfer to the prepared baking dish. Top with the marshmallows.

Bake until the marshmallows are golden brown, about 30 minutes.

4 TO 6 SERVINGS
PREP TIME: 15 MINUTES
COOK TIME: 55 MINUTES

TIP

Use leftovers to make shortcakes on page 79.

simmered collard greens

We always ate greens when I was a kid. Kale, turnip greens, dandelion greens, collards—I loved them all. Most people put a ham hock or bacon in their greens, but I think it's overpowering. My favorite way to prepare them is to simmer the greens in chicken broth flavored with soy sauce. I put a bottle of hot pepper vinegar on the table and let people spice up their greens if they like.

3 BUNCHES COLLARD GREENS

1 TABLESPOON OLIVE OIL

½ ONION, THINLY SLICED

2 CUPS LOW-SODIUM CHICKEN BROTH

2 TABLESPOONS SOY SAUCE

¼ TEASPOON GARLIC POWDER

½ TEASPOON KOSHER SALT

½ TEASPOON FRESHLY GROUND BLACK PEPPER

1 TABLESPOON APPLE CIDER VINEGAR

HOT PEPPER VINEGAR, OPTIONAL

Remove the white rib from center of the collards leaves. Stack the leaves on top of each other and slice into 1-inch pieces. Thoroughly wash the greens. (I soak them and continue to change water until no dirt or sand remains.) Set aside.

Heat the olive oil in a Dutch oven over medium heat. Add the onions and cook until translucent, about 5 minutes. Pour in the chicken broth and use a wooden spoon to scrape up any brown bits. Stir in the soy sauce, garlic powder, salt, and pepper. Bring to a low boil. Add the greens and reduce the heat to very a low simmer. Cover and let cook, stirring occasionally, for 1 hour. Stir in the vinegar and simmer an additional 15 minutes. Serve with hot pepper vinegar, if desired.

4 TO 6 SERVINGS
PREP TIME: 20 MINUTES
COOK TIME: 1 HOUR 20 MINUTES

frozen southsiders

The first time I had a Southsider was at a friend's house in Palm Beach. The drink is traditionally shaken and served on the rocks, but she made hers in a blender with ice. I was hooked. I went online to learn about the history of my new favorite drink—there are all kinds of claims to its origination. Some say it started in Prohibition-era Chicago before becoming a favorite of the country-club set; others say the 21 Club in New York City created it. Whatever its provenance, this storied cocktail is refreshing and delicious.

Place all ingredients in a blender. Blend until smooth. Serve in goblets.

4 TO 6 COCKTAILS (ABOUT 6 CUPS)
PREP TIME: 3 MINUTES

6 OUNCES GIN

2 CUPS LEMONADE

2 CUPS ICE

20 FRESH MINT LEAVES

chocolate banana cream pie

The combination of chocolate and bananas is one of my favorites. The rich chocolate pudding with the sweet sliced bananas and the light whipped cream with the salty crust just puts me over the edge. This pie is so heavenly it will disappear in minutes. I suggest cutting a piece for yourself and hiding it in the fridge for leftovers before you serve it.

Preheat the oven to 425°F.

Place the pie crust in a pie plate and pinch the edges to create a rim. Use a fork to prick holes in the dough. Fill the crust with pie weights or beans. Bake 15 minutes. Remove the pie weights. Reduce the oven temperature to 375°F and bake an additional 15 to 20 minutes, until golden brown. Let cool completely.

While the crust is cooling, in a medium saucepan over medium heat, combine the white sugar, cocoa, flour, and salt. Mix well. Whisk in the milk. Stir constantly with a wooden spoon while the mixture comes to a low boil and becomes thick, 5 to 7 minutes. Reduce the heat to very low. Stir a couple of tablespoons of the hot mixture into the egg yolks. Stir the egg yolks back into the hot milk mixture. Stir constantly until thickened, 3 to 4 minutes. Remove from the heat and stir in 1 teaspoon of the vanilla extract.

Line the crust with half of the banana slices. Pour the pudding into the pie crust. Top with the remaining banana

ONE 9-INCH PIE CRUST (STORE-BOUGHT OR HOMEMADE)

½ CUP WHITE SUGAR

½ CUP HIGH-QUALITY COCOA POWDER

¼ CUP ALL-PURPOSE FLOUR

¼ TEASPOON KOSHER SALT

2 CUPS WHOLE MILK

3 EXTRA LARGE EGG YOLKS, LIGHTLY BEATEN

2 TEASPOONS VANILLA EXTRACT

2 RIPE BANANAS, THINLY SLICED ON DIAGONAL

1 CUP HEAVY CREAM

2 TABLESPOONS CONFECTIONERS' SUGAR

CHOCOLATE SHAVINGS, FOR GARNISH

SPECIAL EQUIPMENT: PIE WEIGHTS OR DRY BEANS

continued

slices. Cover with plastic wrap and refrigerate until chilled, about 2 hours.

Using an electric mixer on high speed, beat the cream, confectioners' sugar, and remaining 1 teaspoon vanilla until stiff peaks form. Spread the whipped cream on the pie. Top with chocolate shavings. Refrigerate until serving time.

6 TO 8 SERVINGS
PREP TIME: 20 MINUTES
INACTIVE PREP TIME: 2 HOURS TO CHILL PIE
COOK TIME: 45 MINUTES

chrismukkah

About half of my friends celebrate Hanukkah and the other half celebrate Christmas. Last year, I decided to throw a holiday party combining the two (à la Seth Cohen in *The O.C.*) and it was a great success. I served foods that were traditional to both holidays, like latkes and Christmas cookies, and I opted to make fish the main course so there would be no issue of the combination of meat and dairy for those who kept kosher. During cocktail hour, we trimmed the Christmas tree in Hanukkah colors of blue and silver and lit the menorah. All in all, it was one of the most fun parties I have ever had. People didn't leave until well after midnight!

MENU

MINI POTATO-LEEK LATKES
WITH SPICY APPLE CHUTNEY

WILD MUSHROOM SOUP "CAPPUCCINO"

HERB-ROASTED SALMON

STEWED FRENCH LENTILS

SPINACH AND THREE-CHEESE PHYLLO PIE

TRIPLE CHOCOLATE BROWNIES

MEXICAN WEDDING COOKIES

CAMPARI AND BLOOD ORANGE SPARKLERS

SERVES 12 TO 14

WINE

Pinot Noir

PLAYLIST

A Charlie Brown Christmas · BY VINCE GUARALDI TRIO
"Little St. Nick" · BY BEACH BOYS
"Santa Baby" · BY EARTHA KITT
"Christmas, Baby Please Come Home" · BY U2
"Winter Wonderland" · BY CYNDI LAUPER
"Hannukah Song" · BY ADAM SANDLER

mini potato-leek latkes with spicy apple chutney

Latkes for Hanukkah are a *must*. The story of Hanukkah celebrates the miracle of a small can of oil burning for eight days, so frying food (like latkes) in oil is symbolic. It's traditional to serve latkes with applesauce, so I decided to put my own spin on it with this spicy apple chutney. I make these small so they can be consumed in one or two bites, but you can make them bigger if you like.

FOR THE LATKES

Press the excess water from the grated potatoes. In a medium bowl, mix the potatoes with the leeks, eggs, bread crumbs, parsley, salt, and pepper.

In a large heavy skillet over medium heat, melt the butter with the oil. Use a tablespoon to drop potato batter into the skillet. Flatten the potatoes with a spatula. Fry until golden brown, a couple minutes on each side. Drain on paper towels and serve immediately.

FOR THE CHUTNEY

In a small bowl, combine the orange juice, water, brown sugar, vinegar, cinnamon, salt, and pepper.

Heat the olive oil in a small saucepan over medium heat. Add the shallots, garlic, and jalapeño and sauté about 5 minutes. Stir in the apples and orange juice mixture. Let come to a low simmer. Cover and cook until apples are tender, stirring occasionally, about 8 to 10 minutes. Serve with the latkes.

12 TO 14 SERVINGS
PREP TIME: 20 MINUTES
COOK TIME: 30 MINUTES

For the latkes

3 LARGE BAKING POTATOES, PEELED AND GRATED

½ CUP FINELY DICED LEEKS, WHITE PART ONLY

3 LARGE EGGS, LIGHTLY BEATEN

½ CUP DRY BREAD CRUMBS

2 TABLESPOONS MINCED FLAT-LEAF PARSLEY

1½ TEASPOONS KOSHER SALT

½ TEASPOON FRESHLY GROUND BLACK PEPPER

4 TABLESPOONS (½ STICK) UNSALTED BUTTER

¼ CUP CANOLA OIL

For the chutney

¼ CUP ORANGE JUICE

¼ CUP WATER

3 TABLESPOONS LIGHT BROWN SUGAR

3 TABLESPOONS APPLE CIDER VINEGAR

½ TEASPOON GROUND CINNAMON

½ TEASPOON KOSHER SALT

¼ TEASPOON FRESHLY GROUND BLACK PEPPER

2 TEASPOONS OLIVE OIL

2 SHALLOTS, MINCED

1 GARLIC CLOVE, MINCED

½ JALAPEÑO, MINCED

2 GRANNY SMITH APPLES, PEELED, CORED, AND DICED

wild mushroom soup "cappuccino"

Soup makes for a festive party hors d'oeuvre when served in a small vessel. I serve this wild mushroom soup in an espresso cup with a dollop of crème fraîche so that it looks like a frothy cappuccino. It's something a little different than the usual canapé and tastes great. Note that this recipe only makes enough for fourteen espresso cups, so if you plan on serving it in soup cups, be sure to double the recipe.

2 TABLESPOONS ($\frac{1}{4}$ STICK) UNSALTED BUTTER

1 YELLOW ONION, FINELY DICED

1 GARLIC CLOVE, MINCED

1 BAY LEAF

3 CUPS FINELY DICED MIXED WILD MUSHROOMS

2 TABLESPOONS ALL-PURPOSE FLOUR

1$\frac{1}{2}$ TEASPOONS KOSHER SALT

1 TEASPOON FRESHLY GROUND BLACK PEPPER

6 CUPS VEGETABLE BROTH

1 CUP HEAVY CREAM

CRÈME FRAÎCHE AND MINCED FLAT-LEAF PARSLEY, FOR GARNISH

In a Dutch oven over medium heat, melt the butter. Add the onion, garlic, and bay leaf. Cook until the onions are translucent, about 10 minutes. Add the mushrooms and cook until tender and any moisture has evaporated.

Stir in the flour, salt, and pepper and cook 2 to 3 minutes. Add the vegetable broth and bring to a low boil. Reduce the heat to a simmer, cover, and cook 20 minutes. Stir in the cream and cook an additional 10 minutes, stirring often.

Serve in espresso cups garnished with crème fraîche and parsley.

12 TO 14 SERVINGS (ABOUT 7 CUPS)
PREP TIME: 15 MINUTES
COOK TIME: 50 MINUTES

herb-roasted salmon

Serving a side of salmon is one of the easiest ways to feed a crowd. For twelve to fourteen people, two sides are necessary, but this recipe is easily halved if you want to make it for a smaller party. It is just as delicious as leftovers the next day for lunch—I like it chilled with a salad.

Preheat oven to 450°F. Line a baking sheet with parchment paper.

In a medium bowl, combine the herbs, sugar, mustard, salt, and pepper.

Place salmon on the baking sheet, skin side down. Spread the herb mixture evenly on each piece of salmon. Top salmon with lemon slices.

Bake about 15 to 20 minutes, until the salmon is just opaque in the center. Use the parchment paper to help transfer the sides of salmon to a serving platter.

12 TO 14 SERVINGS
PREP TIME: 10 MINUTES
COOK TIME: 20 MINUTES

3 CUPS LOOSELY PACKED MIXED FRESH HERBS, MINCED (I LIKE A COMBINATION OF FLAT-LEAF PARSLEY, THYME, CHIVES, AND MINT)

½ CUP LIGHT BROWN SUGAR

¼ CUP DIJON MUSTARD

1 TABLESPOON KOSHER SALT

2 TEASPOONS FRESHLY GROUND BLACK PEPPER

TWO 3- TO 3½-POUND WHOLE SIDES OF SALMON WITH SKIN (ABOUT 1½ INCHES THICK AT THE THICK-EST PART)

2 LEMONS, THINLY SLICED

stewed french lentils

Salmon paired with lentils is a very traditional French meal. Not only are lentils tasty and healthy, they are also really inexpensive, making them perfect for a big group. I like serving this recipe for a party because it doesn't require much attention—it's one of those things that can be put on the stove and forgotten about until serving time.

1 TABLESPOON OLIVE OIL

2 CUPS DICED YELLOW ONIONS

2 CUPS DICED CARROTS

1 CUP DICED CELERY

4 GARLIC CLOVES, MINCED

ONE 28-OUNCE CAN DICED TOMATOES

1¼ CUP FRENCH GREEN LENTILS

2 CUPS VEGETABLE BROTH

1 BAY LEAF

1½ TEASPOONS MINCED FRESH
    ROSEMARY

2 TEASPOONS FRESH THYME LEAVES

2 TEASPOONS KOSHER SALT

½ TEASPOON FRESHLY GROUND
    BLACK PEPPER

1 TABLESPOON BALSAMIC VINEGAR

In a large Dutch oven over medium heat, heat the olive oil. Add the onions, carrots, celery, and garlic. Sauté until vegetables are tender, about 10 minutes. Add tomatoes with their juices, the lentils, broth, bay leaf, rosemary, thyme, salt, and pepper. Bring to a low boil, then lower to a simmer. Cover and simmer about 1 hour, stirring occasionally. Stir in the balsamic vinegar. Cook uncovered for an additional 10 minutes. Serve.

12 TO 14 SERVINGS (ABOUT 8 CUPS)
PREP TIME: 20 MINUTES
COOK TIME: 1 HOUR 20 MINUTES

TIP

Serve leftovers with rice.
Delicious and healthy!

spinach and three-cheese phyllo pie

I love spanikopita, but it can be labor intensive. I like to make it in one big rectangular dish, and instead of just using feta cheese, I also add ricotta and Parmesan. I sprinkle the phyllo with za'tar, a traditional spice and sesame seed blend from Israel.

½ CUP PINE NUTS

2 TABLESPOONS (¼ STICK) UNSALTED BUTTER

1 TABLESPOON OLIVE OIL

2 YELLOW ONIONS, DICED

2 GARLIC CLOVES, MINCED

THREE 20-OUNCE BAGS FROZEN CHOPPED SPINACH, THAWED AND SQUEEZED OF EXCESS WATER

4 EXTRA LARGE EGGS, LIGHTLY BEATEN

2 CUPS CRUMBLED FETA CHEESE

1 CUP RICOTTA CHEESE

½ CUP GRATED PARMESAN CHEESE

2 TEASPOONS KOSHER SALT

1 TEASPOON FRESHLY GROUND BLACK PEPPER

1 TEASPOON GROUND NUTMEG

8 SHEETS PHYLLO DOUGH, THAWED

3 TABLESPOONS UNSALTED BUTTER, MELTED

2 TEASPOONS ZA'TAR (IF YOU CAN'T FIND ZA'TAR, USE SESAME SEEDS)

Preheat the oven to 375°F. Grease a 13 by 9-inch baking dish.

In a large dry skillet over medium heat, lightly toast the pine nuts. Remove and reserve. Melt the butter with the olive oil. Add the onions and sauté until translucent, about 10 minutes. Add the garlic and sauté 2 to 3 minutes. Stir in the spinach. Cook until tender and any excess water evaporates, about 5 minutes. Remove from heat and let cool.

In a large bowl, mix the eggs, feta, ricotta, Parmesan, pine nuts, salt, pepper, and nutmeg. Add the reserved spinach mixture and stir to combine. Transfer to the baking dish.

Layer sheets of phyllo onto the spinach, brushing each sheet with melted butter before adding the next. Fold the edges to make a crust and brush with butter. Sprinkle with za'tar or sesame seeds. Bake until golden brown, about 55 to 60 minutes.

12 TO 14 SERVINGS
PREP TIME: 30 MINUTES
INACTIVE PREP TIME: 20 MINUTES TO COOL SPINACH
COOK TIME: 1 HOUR PLUS 25 MINUTES

triple chocolate brownies

Okay, what's not to love about the sound of these? I'm a self-confessed chocaholic and I have to be watched like a hawk around these or else they might disappear. Great on their own, or incredibly decadent when topped with ice cream and hot fudge for the ultimate brownie sundae!

Preheat the oven to 350°F. Grease an 8 by 8-inch square baking dish.

In a small saucepan over low heat, melt the unsweetened chocolate, butter, and cocoa powder, stirring constantly. Remove from heat and set aside.

In a medium bowl, sift the flour, baking powder, and salt. Set aside.

In a large bowl, beat the eggs and sugar until thick and pale, about 5 minutes. Add the chocolate mixture and vanilla and mix well. Stir in the flour until blended. Add the chocolate chips and stir. Bake for 40 to 45 minutes, until brownies just begin to pull away from the sides of the pan. Let cool. Cut into squares and serve.

12 SERVINGS
PREP TIME: 20 MINUTES
COOK TIME: 40 MINUTES

4 OUNCES (4 SQUARES) UNSWEET-ENED CHOCOLATE

8 TABLESPOONS (1 STICK) UNSALTED BUTTER

½ CUP COCOA POWDER

¾ CUP ALL-PURPOSE FLOUR

½ TEASPOON BAKING POWDER

¼ TEASPOON SALT

3 EXTRA LARGE EGGS

1½ CUPS SUGAR

1 TEASPOON VANILLA EXTRACT

1 CUP SEMISWEET CHOCOLATE CHIPS

mexican wedding cookies

It wouldn't be the holidays at our house without these cookies. My great-aunt, Pat, makes these every year and puts them in tins as gifts. They are simply delicious. I make mine with ground pecans, but you can substitute almonds or walnuts instead. They are excellent with coffee or tea and can really be made any time of year. I nicknamed them snowballs because that's what they look like.

$\frac{1}{2}$ POUND (2 STICKS) UNSALTED BUTTER, AT ROOM TEMPERATURE

$2\frac{1}{2}$ CUPS CONFECTIONERS' SUGAR

1 TEASPOON VANILLA EXTRACT

$2\frac{1}{2}$ CUPS ALL-PURPOSE FLOUR

$\frac{1}{4}$ TEASPOON SALT

$\frac{1}{2}$ TEASPOON GROUND CINNAMON

1 CUP PECANS, GROUND

With an electric mixer, beat the butter and ½ cup confectioners' sugar. Add the vanilla. Stir in the flour, salt, cinnamon, and pecans. Form the dough into a ball and cover with plastic wrap. Chill for 1 hour.

Preheat oven to 375°F.

Roll the dough into 1-inch balls. (The dough may be a bit crumbly.) Place on the baking sheets. Bake for 15 minutes. Cool on a wire rack.

Roll each cookie in the remaining confectioners' sugar. Let sit 15 minutes then roll a second time. Store in airtight container.

ABOUT 5 DOZEN COOKIES
PREP TIME: 40 MINUTES
INACTIVE PREP TIME: 1 HOUR, PLUS 15 MINUTES
COOK TIME: 15 MINUTES

campari and blood orange sparklers

Bubbles make any occasion special. These sparklers are particularly merry because of the bright color created by the Campari and blood orange juice. Blood oranges are in season in the winter, but this recipe will work just fine with regular oranges if you need to substitute.

2 OUNCES FRESH BLOOD ORANGE JUICE

$\frac{1}{4}$ TO $\frac{1}{2}$ CUP SUGAR IN A SMALL SHALLOW DISH, FOR RIMMING THE GLASSES

1 OUNCE CAMPARI

SPARKLING WINE

Press a slice of a juiced blood orange (or a damp paper towel) around the rim of a champagne glass. Press the top of the glass in the sugar to coat the rim.

Combine the blood orange juice and Campari in the champagne glass. Top with sparkling wine.

1 COCKTAIL
PREP TIME: 2 MINUTES

baby, it's cold outside

I'm not much of a cold weather person, so when the temperature drops, I stay inside. The only thing that gets me through the winter is comfort food. On those freezing cold days, there's nothing I love more than putting a pot roast in the oven and letting its aroma fill the house. Turn on some good music, light a fire, open a bottle of red, and watch the snow fall until dinner is ready.

MENU

FENNEL SALAD WITH RED ONIONS
AND ORANGES

POT ROAST

CHIVE-BUTTERED EGG NOODLES

LARRY'S FAVORITE PRUNE CAKE

BOURBON SOUR

SERVES 6 TO 8

WINE

Cabernet Sauvignon

PLAYLIST

"Beast of Burden" • BY THE ROLLING STONES
"Tuesdays Gone" • BY LYNYRD SKYNYRD
"Layla" • BY DEREK AND THE DOMINOS
"Lay Lady Lay" • BY BOB DYLAN
"Mona Lisas and Mad Hatters" • BY ELTON JOHN
"And It Stoned Me" • BY VAN MORRISON

fennel salad with red onions and oranges

Fennel is so crisp and refreshing. Its anisette flavor is perfect with the red onions and sweet orange segments. I dress this salad simply with extra virgin olive oil, lemon juice, and just a little salt and pepper. It's just right served with something heavy like pot roast.

3 FENNEL BULBS, CORED, TRIMMED, AND VERY THINLY SLICED

1 TABLESPOON CHOPPED FENNEL FRONDS

½ RED ONION, VERY THINLY SLICED

1 ORANGE, PEELED AND CUT INTO SEGMENTS

2 TABLESPOONS EXTRA VIRGIN OLIVE OIL

2 TABLESPOONS FRESH LEMON JUICE

KOSHER SALT AND FRESHLY GROUND BLACK PEPPER

In a large bowl, toss fennel, fronds, onion, and orange with olive oil and lemon juice. Season with salt and pepper.

6 TO 8 SERVINGS
PREP TIME: 15 MINUTES

pot roast

People always ask me what my favorite comfort food is, and it just might be pot roast. For me, there's nothing better on a cold day than a hearty pot roast. The house will smell so good with it slowly cooking in the oven all day. Serve it with the delicate chive-buttered noodles or with mashed potatoes.

Preheat the oven to 300°F. Season all sides of chuck roast with 1 tablespoon kosher salt and 2 teaspoons black pepper. Dredge in flour.

In a large Dutch oven, heat the canola oil over medium-high heat. Brown the roast on all sides, 4 to 5 minutes per side. Remove the roast from the Dutch oven and set aside. Reduce the heat to medium and add the onions, carrots, leeks, mushrooms, and garlic. Cook, stirring occasionally, for about 5 minutes. Add the wine and use a wooden spoon to scrape up any browned bits. Stir in the broth, tomato paste, and the remaining salt and pepper. Place the roast in the center of the Dutch oven and nestle it in the broth and vegetables. Bring the liquid to a low boil. Cover and put in the oven. Cook for 3 to 3½ hours, until the beef is fork tender.

Remove the roast to a cutting board. Remove the strings. Slice and serve over buttered egg noodles. Spoon the pan juices and vegetables over the beef and noodles, if desired. Serve immediately.

6 TO 8 SERVINGS
PREP TIME: 30 MINUTES
COOK TIME: 4 HOURS

ONE 4- TO 5-POUND CHUCK ROAST, TIED

1 TABLESPOON PLUS 1 TEASPOON KOSHER SALT

2 TEASPOONS PLUS ½ TEASPOON FRESHLY GROUND BLACK PEPPER

¼ CUP ALL-PURPOSE FLOUR

2 TABLESPOONS CANOLA OIL

2 LARGE ONIONS, PEELED AND QUARTERED

4 LARGE CARROTS, SPLIT LENGTHWISE AND CUT INTO 1½-INCH PIECES

2 LARGE LEEKS, LIGHT GREEN AND WHITE PARTS, SLICED

2 CUPS WHITE BUTTON MUSHROOMS, SLICED

2 WHOLE PEELED GARLIC CLOVES

1 CUP RED WINE

1 QUART BEEF BROTH

2 TABLESPOONS TOMATO PASTE

chive-buttered egg noodles

These are so easy and delicious! The chives add just the right touch of flavor and a beautiful bright green color.

ONE 12-OUNCE PACKAGE EGG
    NOODLES
3 TABLESPOONS UNSALTED BUTTER,
    AT ROOM TEMPERATURE
3 TABLESPOONS MINCED CHIVES
KOSHER SALT AND FRESHLY
    GROUND BLACK PEPPER

Bring a large pot of salted water to a boil. Cook the noodles according to package directions, reserving ¼ cup cooking water. Toss the noodles with reserved water, butter, chives, and season with salt and pepper.

6 TO 8 SERVINGS
PREP TIME: 5 MINUTES
COOK TIME: ABOUT 10 MINUTES

larry's favorite prune cake

My great-uncle Larry loved this prune cake. I always say that food has the power to evoke memories and emotion. We all miss him so much and every time someone in our family makes this cake, we think of him.

For the cake

2 CUPS ALL-PURPOSE FLOUR

1 TEASPOON BAKING SODA

½ TEASPOON SALT

1 TEASPOON GROUND CINNAMON

1 TEASPOON GROUND NUTMEG

1 TEASPOON GROUND ALLSPICE

½ CUP CANOLA OIL

1 CUP SUGAR

3 EXTRA LARGE EGGS

1 TEASPOON VANILLA EXTRACT

1 CUP BUTTERMILK

1 CUP CHOPPED COOKED PRUNES
(CANNED PRUNES ARE FINE,
DRAINED AND RINSED)

1 CUP CHOPPED WALNUTS

For the glaze

½ CUP SUGAR

2 TABLESPOONS BUTTERMILK

2 TABLESPOONS (¼ STICK) UNSALTED
BUTTER

1 TABLESPOON MAPLE SYRUP

½ TEASPOON VANILLA EXTRACT

FOR THE CAKE

Preheat oven to 325°F. Grease and flour a Bundt pan.

In a medium bowl, combine the flour, baking soda, salt, cinnamon, nutmeg, and allspice. In a large bowl, beat the oil, sugar, and eggs until light and fluffy, about 4 minutes. Add the vanilla and mix to combine. Add the flour mixture alternately with buttermilk, stirring until combined. Stir in the prunes and walnuts. Pour into the prepared pan. Bake 60 to 65 minutes. Invert the cake onto a cooling rack placed over a baking sheet.

FOR THE GLAZE

In a small saucepan over medium heat, combine all the ingredients and bring to a low boil, stirring constantly. Cook until the sugar is dissolved, 2 to 3 minutes.

Gently spoon the hot glaze over the cake to coat. If necessary, collect the drippings and spoon over the cake again.

6 TO 8 SERVINGS
PREP TIME: 20 MINUTES
INACTIVE PREP TIME: 20 MINUTES TO COOL
   CAKE
COOK TIME: 65 MINUTES

TIP

Tastes great in the afternon
with a cup of tea..

bourbon sour

Mmmm...just the thought of a bourbon sour makes my mouth pucker and I feel warm and fuzzy all over. It's the perfect drink to heat up a cold winter day, but it's also ideal to cool off in the summer. I make mine with honey, but simple syrup also works nicely to add a touch of sweetness.

2 OUNCES BOURBON

1 OUNCE FRESH LEMON JUICE

½ OUNCE HONEY

ORANGE SLICE

MARASCHINO CHERRY

Combine the bourbon, lemon juice, and honey in a cocktail shaker filled with ice. Shake vigorously. Strain into a rocks glass filled with ice and garnish with an orange slice and a maraschino cherry.

1 COCKTAIL
PREP TIME: 2 MINUTES

baby, it's cold outside

chinese new year

Whenever it's been a long day and I don't feel like cooking, I order Chinese take-out. Growing up in West Virginia, I was never really exposed to Chinese food much, but since moving to New York City, it has quickly become a staple in my diet.

The New Year is the most important holiday in the Chinese calendar. The holiday is marked by celebrations and large feasts. People wear red, which according to legend symbolizes fire and drives away bad luck.

I enjoy inviting friends for a Chinese New Year feast at home and I serve a family-style meal of traditional foods. I decorate with paper lanterns and pick up fortune cookies from my local Chinese restaurant. It always proves to be a fun and festive evening.

MENU

SHRIMP POTSTICKERS WITH
GINGER-LEMON DIPPING SAUCE

CHICKEN LETTUCE CUPS

CRISPY ORANGE BEEF

LONG LIFE NOODLES

STIR-FRIED BROCCOLI
WITH GARLIC AND CHILI

CHINESE FIVE-SPICE KETTLE CORN

MAI TAI COCKTAIL

SERVES 6 TO 8

WINE

Sangiovese
Barbera
Riesling

PLAYLIST

"Change" • *by Joy Denalane* FEATURING LUPE FIASCO
"One Evening (Remix by VV)" • BY FEIST
"California Soul (Diplo/Mad Decent Remix)"
BY MARLENA SHAW
"The World Should Revolve Around Me"
BY LITTLE JACKIE
"Dream Machine (Downtempo Mix)"
BY MARK FARINA

shrimp potstickers with ginger-lemon dipping sauce

Making homemade potstickers is much easier than you'd think, and the little extra effort is well worth it in the end. Store-bought wonton wrappers are very easy to work with and once assembled, these potstickers can be refrigerated or frozen until you are ready to use them. I like to take any uncooked potstickers and drop them in boiling chicken broth combined with the leftover dipping sauce for an instant wonton soup.

FOR THE POTSTICKERS

In a food processor, pulse shrimp until ground. Transfer to a mixing bowl. Add the scallions, egg, salt, and pepper, and using your hands, mix thoroughly.

Place 1 level teaspoon of the shrimp mixture onto each wonton. Brush the edge with water and fold into a half moon to seal. Cover with a damp paper towel.

In a large skillet, heat 2 tablespoons of the oil over medium high heat. Add half of the dumplings and cook 2 minutes. Add 2 tablespoons water, cover, and let steam 3 to 4 minutes. Cook the dumpling a few minutes longer with the lid off if they are sticking to the pan. Repeat with other half of dumplings.

FOR THE DIPPING SAUCE

Whisk the soy sauce, lemon juice, ginger, barbecue sauce, and sesame oil. Stir in the scallions.

6 TO 8 SERVINGS
PREP TIME: 25 MINUTES
COOK TIME: 12 MINUTES

For the potstickers

$1/2$ POUND SHRIMP, PEELED AND DEVEINED

$1/4$ CUP THINLY SLICED SCALLIONS

1 LARGE EGG, LIGHTLY BEATEN

$1/2$ TEASPOON KOSHER SALT

$1/4$ TEASPOON FRESHLY GROUND BLACK PEPPER

24 TO 30 ROUND WONTON OR GYOZA WRAPPERS

$1/4$ CUP CANOLA OIL

$1/4$ CUP WATER

For the dipping sauce

2 TABLESPOONS SOY SAUCE

3 TABLESPOONS FRESH LEMON JUICE

1 TEASPOON GRATED FRESH GINGER

1 TABLESPOON BBQ SAUCE (PAGE 245)

1 TEASPOON TOASTED SESAME OIL

1 SCALLION, THINLY SLICED

chicken lettuce cups

The first time I made these, I stood over the stove with a spoon, and ate almost the whole thing straight out of the pan—it's that good. The mint and cilantro garnishes add so much flavor, and the lettuce cup adds a refreshing crunch to the spicy chicken.

1 PACKET STIR-FRY SEASONING POWDER

¼ CUP WATER

2 TABLESPOONS SOY SAUCE

2 TABLESPOONS FRESH LIME JUICE

1 TEASPOON SUGAR

1 TABLESPOON CANOLA OIL

1 POUND GROUND CHICKEN BREAST

1 RED BELL PEPPER, DICED

¼ CUP DICED WATER CHESTNUTS

2 TABLESPOONS THINLY SLICED SCALLIONS

PINCH OF RED PEPPER FLAKES

1 HEAD OF ROMAINE LETTUCE (INNER LEAVES ONLY), OR 2 HEADS BUTTER LETTUCE OR RADICCHIO

MINCED MINT AND CILANTRO, BEAN SPROUTS, AND CHOPPED PEA-NUTS, FOR GARNISH

In a small bowl, combine the stir-fry seasoning, water, soy sauce, lime juice, and sugar. Set aside.

Heat oil in a large skillet over medium heat. Add chicken and use a wooden spoon to break up the meat. Cook until browned, about 10 minutes. Add the red bell pepper, water chestnuts, scallions, and red pepper flakes and cook 5 minutes. Stir in reserved stir-fry seasoning mix. Cook until liquid evaporates, 2 to 3 minutes.

Spoon chicken mixture into lettuce cups and garnish with mint, cilantro, bean sprouts, and chopped peanuts.

**6 TO 8 SERVINGS
(ABOUT 8 TO 12 LETTUCE CUPS)**
PREP TIME: 25 MINUTES
COOK TIME: 20 MINUTES

crispy orange beef

I always order orange beef at Chinese restaurants, so I wanted to try making my own at home. It tastes so good that I usually just make it for myself now instead of dialing up for take-out! This is a visually appealing dish as well with the orange peel and green scallions, perfect for a Chinese New Year party. Bonus: Chinese tradition says that oranges represent wealth and good fortune—and we could all use some of that!

3 POUNDS FLANK STEAK, CUT INTO THIN STRIPS

⅓ CUP CORNSTARCH

6 TABLESPOONS SOY SAUCE

2 TABLESPOONS RICE VINEGAR

2 TABLESPOONS HOISIN SAUCE

2 TABLESPOONS HONEY

4 TEASPOONS TOASTED SESAME OIL

½ TEASPOON RED PEPPER FLAKES

½ CUP WATER

1 CUP CANOLA OIL

8 GARLIC CLOVES, MINCED

2 TABLESPOONS GRATED FRESH GINGER

¼ CUP MINCED ORANGE PEEL (PITH REMOVED)

8 SCALLIONS, WHITE AND GREEN PARTS, THINLY SLICED

STEAMED RICE, FOR SERVING

1 ORANGE, THINLY SLICED, FOR GARNISH

Toss beef with cornstarch to evenly coat. Refrigerate for 30 minutes.

In the meantime, in a small bowl, combine the soy sauce, vinegar, hoisin sauce, honey, sesame oil, red pepper flakes, and water. Set aside.

In a wok or heavy skillet, heat the canola oil. Fry the beef, in batches, until browned, about 3 minutes each batch. Remove and let drain on paper towels.

Drain all but 2 tablespoons oil from the wok. Heat the oil over medium heat and add the garlic, ginger, orange peel, and scallions and stir-fry for 5 minutes. Add the beef and stir in the sauce. Raise the heat to medium-high and stir until sauce thickens. Serve over steamed rice with the orange slices on top.

6 TO 8 SERVINGS
PREP TIME: 20 MINUTES
INACTIVE PREP TIME: 30 MINUTES
COOK TIME: 15 MINUTES

long life noodles

Long life noodles, or longevity noodles, are a traditional Chinese dish for both birthdays and New Year. As their name indicates, these noodles symbolize living well into old age. Whatever you do, don't break them or cut them, as it is considered bad luck to do so.

½ CUP CREAMY SALTED PEANUT BUTTER

⅓ CUP SOY SAUCE

¼ CUP RICE VINEGAR

2 TABLESPOONS FRESH LIME JUICE

2 TEASPOONS TOASTED SESAME OIL

2 GARLIC CLOVES, MINCED

1 TEASPOON GRATED FRESH GINGER

1 CUP SNOW PEAS, THINLY SLICED

1 CUP SHREDDED CARROTS

1 RED BELL PEPPER, THINLY SLICED

4 SCALLIONS, THINLY SLICED

1 POUND SOBA NOODLES OR SPAGHETTI

2 TABLESPOONS SESAME SEEDS

¼ CUP MINCED CILANTRO

In a small saucepan over low heat, combine the peanut butter, soy sauce, vinegar, lime juice, sesame oil, garlic, and ginger. Stir constantly until the peanut butter melts. Remove from the heat and set aside.

In a large bowl, combine the snow peas, carrots, red bell pepper, and scallions.

Cook the noodles until al dente in a large pot of salted boiling water. Reserve ¼ cup cooking water. Stir the noodles into the vegetable mixture and add the peanut sauce. If sauce is too thick, add a little cooking water. Garnish with sesame seeds and cilantro.

6 TO 8 SERVINGS (ABOUT 8 CUPS)
PREP TIME: 20 MINUTES
COOK TIME: 15 MINUTES

stir-fried broccoli with garlic and chili

This broccoli makes a great side dish as it is light but flavorful.

1 TABLESPOON CANOLA OIL

3 GARLIC CLOVES, THINLY SLICED

1/4 TEASPOON RED PEPPER FLAKES

1 POUND BROCCOLI FLORETS

3/4 CUP LOW-SODIUM CHICKEN
   BROTH

1 1/2 TABLESPOONS SOY SAUCE

1/2 TEASPOON FRESHLY GROUND
   BLACK PEPPER

Heat the canola oil over medium-low heat in a wok or large skillet. Add the garlic and red pepper flakes. Let garlic and red pepper flakes infuse the oil for 3 to 4 minutes. Increase the heat to medium and add the broccoli. Stir-fry for 3 to 4 minutes. Add the stock, soy sauce, and black pepper, and cook uncovered for about 5 minutes, until broccoli is tender and almost all the liquid has evaporated.

6 TO 8 SERVINGS
PREP TIME: 5 MINUTES
COOK TIME: 15 MINUTES

chinese five-spice kettle corn

I eat popcorn almost every night, and I like to experiment with different flavors. I make this Chinese Five-Spice Kettle Corn to enjoy with cocktails, and also package it up in take-out boxes as a party favor for my guests.

In a large pot or stockpot with a tight-fitting lid over medium heat, combine the popcorn, oil, sugar, five-spice powder, and salt. Shake constantly. When the popcorn begins to pop, lower the heat to medium-low. Continue to shake until the popping begins to slow. Transfer to a bowl. Drizzle with the melted butter.

¾ CUP POPCORN KERNELS

¼ CUP CANOLA OIL

3 TABLESPOONS SUGAR

2 TABLESPOONS CHINESE FIVE-SPICE POWDER

2 TEASPOONS KOSHER SALT

2 TABLESPOONS (¼ STICK) UNSALTED BUTTER, MELTED

6 TO 8 SERVINGS
PREP TIME: 5 MINUTES
COOK TIME: 5 MINUTES

TIP

Try substituting other spices with this recipe to customize kettle corn flavors

mai tai cocktail

Mai Tais are like a vacation in a glass—I feel like I'm sunning myself on an island in the South Seas. Bali Hai!

1½ OUNCES WHITE RUM

2 OUNCES FRESH ORANGE JUICE

2 OUNCES PINEAPPLE JUICE

1 OUNCE GRENADINE

JUICE OF ½ LIME

Pour rum, orange juice, pineapple juice, grenadine, and lime juice into a cocktail shaker filled with ice. Shake vigorously for 15 seconds. Strain into a rocks glass filled with ice.

1 COCKTAIL
PREP TIME: 2 MINUTES

breakfast with friends

Remember when you were a teenager and there was one kid whose house was "the hang"? Everyone would congregate there before and after the big dance and the mom always had the fridge stocked with plenty of yummy snacks and soda. Well, that's what my house is like now. Only we're not teenagers anymore (though sometimes we might act like it).

My house practically has a revolving door, especially on weekends in the summer, so much so that it's earned the nickname Casa Katie B&B. We spend each morning rehashing the events of the night before over an endless pot of coffee and filling up on a big breakfast. We buy all of the New York newspapers, which are more like tabloids on the weekends, and talk and laugh for hours. It's my favorite part of the day.

MENU

GRAPEFRUIT BRÛLÉE

NUTELLA FRENCH TOAST SANDWICHES

BREAKFAST HASH WITH POACHED EGGS

BIG PITCHER OF BLOODY MARYS

SERVES 6 TO 8

WINE

anything with bubbles!

PLAYLIST

"Here Comes the Sun" • BY THE BEATLES
"Take the Long Way Home" • BY SUPERTRAMP
"Take It Easy" • BY THE EAGLES
"Dreams" • BY FLEETWOOD MAC
"Sun Comes Up" • BY JOHN LEGEND

grapefruit brûlée

My grandma makes these for breakfast all the time. I think she started serving grapefruit this way just to get the kids to eat it, but everyone liked it so much that it stuck.

Preheat the broiler. Position an oven rack in the top third of the oven. In a small bowl, stir together the sugar and cinnamon. Halve each grapefruit. Using a pairing knife, cut around the edge of the grapefruit and between the segments.

Arrange the grapefruit halves on a baking sheet or broiler pan. Sprinkle the cinnamon-sugar mixture evenly over the grapefruit halves. Place under the broiler for about 5 minutes, until the sugar is golden brown and bubbly. Keeping the oven door open a bit will help prevent burning. Be sure to watch closely, the sugar will burn quickly.

6 TO 8 SERVINGS
PREP TIME: 10 MINUTES
COOK TIME: 5 MINUTES

$\frac{1}{3}$ CUP SUGAR

2 TABLESPOONS GROUND CINNAMON

3 OR 4 RUBY RED GRAPEFRUITS

nutella french toast sandwiches

This recipe is truly decadent—it's borderline sinful. I love baking French toast in a casserole dish because it's way less work and can even be assembled the night before. I leave a Post-it on the oven with baking instructions. Whoever gets up first is in charge. When the smell of chocolate and hazelnut starts flowing through the house, everyone rouses out of bed.

8 LARGE EGGS

2½ CUPS WHOLE MILK

¼ CUP SUGAR

½ TEASPOON KOSHER SALT

ZEST OF 1 ORANGE

1 TEASPOON VANILLA EXTRACT

1 LOAF BRIOCHE BREAD, SLICED ABOUT ¾-INCH THICK

¾ CUP NUTELLA

3 RIPE BANANAS, SLICED ON A DIAGONAL

In a large bowl, whisk the eggs, milk, sugar, salt, orange zest, and vanilla. Set aside.

Grease a baking dish. Spread half of the bread slices with Nutella and top with bananas and remaining bread slices. Place in the baking dish. Pour egg mixture over the bread and allow it to soak in, at least 20 minutes. (I like to make this the night before, cover it, and store it in the refrigerator until the next morning.)

Preheat the oven to 350°F. Bake for 50 to 55 minutes, until bread is golden brown and puffy. Let stand 10 minutes before serving.

6 TO 8 SERVINGS
PREP TIME: 15 MINUTES
INACTIVE PREP TIME: 20 MINUTES OR UP TO OVERNIGHT
COOK TIME: 55 MINUTES

breakfast with friends

breakfast hash with poached eggs

This recipe was inspired by my friend Todd Thompson, who happens to be the other half of one of my favorite chefs, Giada de Laurentiis. Todd and Giada were staying with us in the Hamptons when he decided to take all of the leftovers in our refrigerator and mix them together in a skillet. He used hamburger, hot dogs, and all sorts of stuff. We all had a little bit of a hangover from the night before, and Todd's breakfast hash was just the cure.

FOR THE HASH

Place the potatoes in a saucepan and cover with cold water. Bring to a boil over high heat. Reduce the heat to low and simmer for 5 minutes. Drain and reserve.

In a large skillet, brown the sausage over medium heat, stirring with a wooden spoon to break up the meat. Transfer to a paper towel–lined plate. Set aside. Drain all but 1 tablespoon of fat from skillet. Add the butter to the pan and melt over medium heat. Add the onions, red bell pepper, and scallions. Sauté until onions are translucent, about 4 minutes. Add the potatoes and gently stir to mix. Cover and cook for 5 minutes without stirring until the potatoes form a nice golden crust. Remove the cover and stir in the parsley, salt, and pepper. Cover and cook an additional 5 minutes. Remove cover and stir in sausage. Continue cooking, if necessary, until potatoes are fork tender. Sprinkle with the Asiago. Spoon mixture onto each plate and top with one or two poached eggs.

For the hash

2 POUNDS UNPEELED POTATOES, CUT IN $\frac{1}{4}$-INCH DICE

1 POUND BULK BREAKFAST SAUSAGE OR ITALIAN SAUSAGE

3 TABLESPOONS UNSALTED BUTTER

$\frac{1}{2}$ RED ONION, MINCED

1 RED BELL PEPPER, CUT IN $\frac{1}{4}$-INCH DICE

4 SCALLIONS, THINLY SLICED

2 TABLESPOONS MINCED FLAT-LEAF PARSLEY

1 TEASPOON KOSHER SALT

$\frac{1}{2}$ TEASPOON FRESHLY GROUND BLACK PEPPER

$\frac{1}{2}$ CUP GRATED ASIAGO CHEESE

continued

For the poached eggs
2 QUARTS WATER
¼ CUP WHITE VINEGAR
8 EGGS

FOR THE POACHED EGGS

In a large pot, combine the water with the vinegar. Bring to a rolling boil. Reduce heat to a bare simmer. Crack an egg and, holding the shell close to the surface of the simmering water, slide it into the pot. Moving quickly, repeat with the remaining eggs. Poach for 2 minutes. Remove each egg with a slotted spoon and drain on a clean, dry dish towel.

6 TO 8 SERVINGS
PREP TIME: 20 MINUTES
COOK TIME: 25 MINUTES

big pitcher of bloody marys

Nothing cures a hangover like a Bloody Mary! This recipe makes a large amount, but if your friends are like mine, they probably won't have just one drink over the course of a long weekend brunch.

In a large pitcher, combine the vegetable juice, vodka, lemon juice, horseradish, celery salt, kosher salt, onion powder, and Tabasco to taste. Chill until serving time. Pour over ice and garnish with a celery stick, olive, and lemon wedge.

8 TO 10 SERVINGS
PREP TIME: 5 MINUTES

ONE 46-OUNCE BOTTLE LOW-SODIUM VEGETABLE JUICE (I LIKE V8)

1 $\frac{1}{2}$ CUPS VODKA

JUICE OF 1 LEMON

2 TEASPOONS PREPARED WHITE HORSERADISH

1 TEASPOON CELERY SALT

$\frac{1}{2}$ TEASPOON KOSHER SALT

$\frac{1}{4}$ TEASPOON ONION POWDER

TABASCO SAUCE

CELERY STICKS, GREEN OLIVES, AND LEMON WEDGES, FOR GARNISH

super bowl

There's really just about anything I'd rather do than spend my Sunday in front of the tube watching a football game, or any sporting event for that matter. Reorganize my sock drawer. Water the plants. Look for split ends. Stare aimlessly at the ceiling. My one exception: the Super Bowl. Men anxiously await the arrival of this sacred sports day the same way I count down the days to the annual shoe sale at Barneys. Their masculinity overflows just like a keg at a frat party. Over-the-top commercials and anything-can-happen halftime performances keep me highly entertained—I barely even take notice of the main event. Super Bowl Sunday is all the justification I need to overly indulge. I like to think of it as the Thanksgiving of junk food.

If I were the betting type, my money would be on the disappearance of these treats before the first touchdown is scored.

MENU

LEMONY CAESAR SALAD

BUFFALO CHICKEN QUESADILLAS

HERBIE'S TACOS

CHILI-CHEESE DIP

HEAVYWEIGHT HOAGIE

CHOCOLATE PEANUT BUTTER BALLS

SERVES 6 TO 8

WINE

Gewürztraminer
Shiraz
Beer, beer,
& more beer!

lemony caesar salad

With all of the heavy foods going on in this menu, a Caesar salad helps to round things out. My Caesar dressing has two lemons so it has a really bright, fresh flavor. If you are squeamish about anchovies, just leave them out and increase the salt, but I think they are really yummy.

Place the romaine in a large salad bowl.

In a food processor, combine the lemon juice, mustard, garlic, anchovies, and egg yolk. Pulse until blended. With the machine running, pour in the olive oil until emulsified. Stir in the Parmesan, pepper, and salt.

Toss dressing and romaine lettuce until evenly coated. Garnish with Parmesan shavings.

6 TO 8 SERVINGS
PREP TIME: 15 MINUTES

1 HEAD OF ROMAINE LETTUCE, TORN INTO BITE-SIZE PIECES

JUICE OF 2 LEMONS, ABOUT 6 TABLESPOONS

1 TABLESPOON DIJON MUSTARD

2 GARLIC CLOVES, PEELED

2 ANCHOVY FILLETS

1 LARGE EGG YOLK

$\frac{1}{2}$ CUP EXTRA VIRGIN OLIVE OIL

$\frac{1}{4}$ CUP GRATED PARMESAN CHEESE

$\frac{1}{2}$ TEASPOON FRESHLY GROUND BLACK PEPPER

$\frac{1}{4}$ TEASPOON KOSHER SALT

PARMESAN SHAVINGS, FOR GARNISH

buffalo chicken quesadillas

I love the spicy flavors of Buffalo chicken wings, but I usually only have them when I'm dining out. Making wings at home can be messy, but by using a store-bought rotisserie chicken with these quesadillas, I get all the same flavors but none of the mess. I like to serve my quesadillas with blue cheese dressing and celery sticks.

1 STORE-BOUGHT ROTISSERIE CHICKEN, SHREDDED (ABOUT 4 CUPS)

¾ CUP BUFFALO WING SAUCE

2 CUPS SHREDDED MONTEREY JACK CHEESE

12 FLOUR TORTILLAS (SOFT TACO SIZE)

BLUE CHEESE DRESSING (PAGE 34) AND CELERY STICKS, FOR SERVING

In a large bowl, combine the chicken and sauce and stir until evenly coated. Add the cheese and toss to combine. Evenly divide chicken mixture on 6 tortillas and top with remaining 6 tortillas.

Heat a large skillet over medium heat and coat with nonstick cooking spray. Cook the quesadillas, one at a time, about 3 to 4 minutes per side, using a spatula to turn. Cut into quarters and serve with blue cheese dressing and celery sticks on the side.

6 TO 8 SERVINGS
PREP TIME: 20 MINUTES
COOK TIME: 50 MINUTES

TIP

These quesadillas are perfect for reheating. Make them in advance and then pop in the oven for a few minutes before serving.

herbie's tacos

My friend Steve made me these tacos, named for his father, Herbie, who taught him the recipe. They are, without a doubt, the best tacos I have ever eaten. His secret ingredient is cheap Italian salad dressing. Amazing. Have an extra napkin handy because, as Steve says, "If they're not dripping down your hands, you didn't do something right."

FOR THE TACO MEAT

In a large skillet over medium-high heat, heat the oil, cilantro, and scallions. Add the chiles and cook 1 minute, stirring constantly. Stir in the turkey, using a wooden spoon to break up the meat. As the meat is browning, stir in the garlic salt and chili powder. When turkey has cooked through, about 8 to 10 minutes, stir in the hot sauce and green sauce. Lower the heat to a simmer. Stir occasionally.

FOR THE SALAD

As the meat simmers, in a large bowl, toss all salad ingredients with the dressing. Refrigerate until needed.

FOR THE SHELLS

Line a baking sheet or large plate with paper towels. In a medium skillet, heat the oil over medium-high heat. When the oil is hot, use tongs to place a tortilla gently in the oil one at a time. After only 5 seconds, in one motion, turn the tortilla over and fold it in half. Cook 20 seconds, flip, and cook an additional 20 seconds. Lift out of the oil and drain on the paper

For the taco meat

2 TABLESPOONS CANOLA OIL

½ CUP MINCED CILANTRO

1 BUNCH SCALLIONS, THINLY SLICED (WHITE AND GREEN PARTS)

ONE 7-OUNCE CAN CHOPPED GREEN CHILES (MEDIUM HEAT)

2 POUNDS GROUND TURKEY

2 TABLESPOONS GARLIC SALT

¼ CUP CHILI POWDER

¼ CUP HOT TACO SAUCE, PLUS MORE FOR SERVING

¼ CUP GREEN TACO SAUCE, PLUS MORE FOR SERVING (RECOMMENDED BRAND IS LA VICTORIA)

For the salad

1 HEAD OF ICEBERG LETTUCE, SHREDDED

1 BUNCH SCALLIONS, THINLY SLICED (WHITE AND GREEN PARTS)

½ CUP MINCED CILANTRO

2 RIPE TOMATOES, CHOPPED

1 AVOCADO, DICED

½ CUP ITALIAN-STYLE VINAIGRETTE DRESSING (I LIKE KEN'S)

For the shells

1 CUP CANOLA OIL

24 WHITE CORN TORTILLAS

continued

herbie's tacos, *continued*

For the garnish
2 CUPS SHREDDED CHEDDAR
    CHEESE

½ CUP SOUR CREAM

towels. Repeat with the remaining tortillas, one at a time. (The shells should not be too crisp when they come out of the oil. If they become too crisp tacos will be difficult to stuff.)

Assemble the tacos by spooning the meat into the shells and topping with cheese, salad, and sour cream.

6 TO 8 SERVINGS (24 TACOS)
PREP TIME: 20 MINUTES
COOK TIME: 25 MINUTES

chili-cheese dip

When I was in college, we used to melt cheese and chili in the microwave on movie nights. I re-created my college junk-food obsession with this chili-cheese dip that only takes a few more minutes than the microwave version. It's so good—seriously, I need to step away from the tortilla chips.

In a medium skillet over medium heat, brown the beef. Remove the beef from the skillet and drain on paper towels. Return to the skillet and add the taco seasoning and salsa. Bring to a simmer and cook uncovered for 10 minutes, stirring occasionally. Drop the heat to very low. Stir in Cheddar and cream cheese and cook until just melted. Serve hot with tortilla chips.

1 POUND GROUND SIRLOIN BEEF

1 PACKET TACO SEASONING

ONE 16-OUNCE JAR SALSA

2 CUPS SHREDDED CHEDDAR CHEESE

4 OUNCES CREAM CHEESE, CUT INTO CUBES

TORTILLA CHIPS, FOR SERVING

6 TO 8 SERVINGS (ABOUT 3 1/2 CUPS)
PREP TIME: 5 MINUTES
COOK TIME: 20 MINUTES

heavyweight hoagie

This is the mother of all hoagies. I use a whole loaf of ciabatta with turkey, ham, and salami, but try mixing it up with roast beef or mortadella. I wrap the sandwich in aluminum foil and put a heavy cast-iron skillet on top for about 30 minutes so that it smashes and is easier to eat, and the flavors really meld together. Serve it on a cutting board and people can just cut their own sandwich.

3 TABLESPOONS UNSALTED BUTTER

3 GARLIC CLOVES, MINCED

2 TABLESPOONS MINCED FLAT-LEAF PARSLEY

1 LOAF CIABATTA, HALVED LENGTHWISE

$\frac{1}{3}$ CUP MAYONNAISE

$\frac{1}{2}$ POUND THINLY SLICED DELI TURKEY

$\frac{1}{2}$ POUND THINLY SLICED DELI HAM

$\frac{1}{4}$ POUND THINLY SLICED SALAMI

$\frac{1}{4}$ POUND THINLY SLICED PROVOLONE

SALT AND FRESHLY GROUND BLACK PEPPER

1 CUP SHREDDED ICEBERG LETTUCE

$\frac{1}{4}$ CUP SLICED HOT BANANA PEPPERS, DRAINED

$\frac{1}{4}$ CUP THINLY SLICED RED ONION

Preheat the broiler.

In a small skillet over low heat, melt the butter with the garlic. Continue to cook over low heat until the garlic begins to soften, 2 to 3 minutes. Add the parsley and cook another minute. Remove from the heat and spread on the inside of each side of the bread. Place under the broiler and toast until golden brown. Let cool.

Spread the mayonnaise onto the bread. Layer the turkey, ham, salami, and provolone on the bottom half of the bread. Sprinkle with salt and pepper. Top with the lettuce, peppers, and onion. Wrap tightly in aluminum foil and place a heavy skillet (I use a cast-iron skillet) on top. Let sit 30 minutes.

Slice and serve.

6 TO 8 SERVINGS
PREP TIME: 10 MINUTES
INACTIVE PREP TIME: 10 MINUTES TO COOL
    BREAD, 30 MINUTES TO PRESS SANDWICH
COOK TIME: 7 MINUTES

chocolate peanut butter balls

My great-aunt Pat makes these peanut butter balls and everyone goes crazy for them. Honestly, I can't sleep at night when they are in my house—I have to eat them. Luckily, they're sure not to last through the big game!

Line a baking sheet with parchment paper.

In a medium saucepan over low heat, melt the butter with the peanut butter. Stir in the vanilla. Remove from the heat. Stir in the sugar until smooth. (The mixture will be the texture of thick dough.) While still warm, use your hands to shape the dough into balls by the tablespoonful. Place on the baking sheet.

In a saucepan over medium-low heat, melt the chocolate, stirring constantly. Remove from the heat and use a toothpick to dip balls halfway in chocolate. Place back on the baking sheet. Refrigerate until set, about 1 hour.

6 TO 8 SERVINGS (ABOUT 42 BALLS)
PREP TIME: 25 MINUTES
INACTIVE PREP TIME: 1 HOUR
COOK TIME: 5 MINUTES

½ POUND (2 STICKS) UNSALTED BUTTER

1 CUP CREAMY PEANUT BUTTER

1 TEASPOON VANILLA EXTRACT

3½ CUPS CONFECTIONERS' SUGAR

8 OUNCES SEMISWEET CHOCOLATE, CHOPPED

TIP

Chocolate Peanut Butter Balls make a great gift. Packaged up in a tin, they are the perfect thank-you or just a great way to let a friend know you love them.

romantic dinner for two

In my opinion, there's no city in the world more romantic than Paris. In the Montparnasse district, there is the most wonderful seafood restaurant, Le Dôme. I eat there on every trip to the City of Lights and I always order the exact same meal. The waiters never change and the service is spot on. I feel as though I'm in a scene from a Nora Ephron movie every time I go there. Paris is so romantic, so when I make this meal at home I imagine I'm sitting at Le Dôme sharing it with the man I love.

MENU

OYSTERS ON THE HALF SHELL WITH
MIGNONETTE SAUCE

SOLE MEUNIÈRE

HERB-ROASTED POTATOES

HARICOTS VERTS WITH GRAPE TOMATOES

RICH CHOCOLATE PUDDING AND AMARETTO
WHIPPED CREAM PARFAITS

CHOCOLATE ROYALE

SERVES 2

WINE

*Champagne
(to start)
Chablis*

PLAYLIST

"How Deep Is Your Love" • BY THE BIRD AND THE BEE
"Kissing" • BY BLISS
"The Scientist" • BY COLDPLAY
"Good Boy" • BY DE-PHAZZ
"Feelin' Love" • BY PAULA COLE

oysters on the half shell with mignonette sauce

Oysters are supposed to be an aphrodisiac. I'm not so sure about that, but I really like eating them. They make for a nice light appetizer paired with a glass of Champagne—perfect for a romantic dinner. Shucking oysters can be difficult, so just ask your fishmonger to do it for you and pack them on ice.

Mix shallots, vinegars, sugar, and pepper until sugar dissolves. Serve oysters on the half shell on a bed of crushed ice, with mignonette sauce on the side and garnished with lemon wedges.

2 SERVINGS
PREP TIME: 15 MINUTES

1 SHALLOT, MINCED

$\frac{1}{4}$ CUP RED WINE VINEGAR

$\frac{1}{4}$ CUP SHERRY VINEGAR

$\frac{1}{4}$ TEASPOON SUGAR

PINCH OF FRESHLY GROUND BLACK PEPPER

8 OYSTERS ON THE HALF SHELL

LEMON WEDGES, FOR GARNISH

sole meunière

This is the signature dish of Le Dôme and a total classic. They use Dover sole, but if you can't find it at your fish market, just substitute sole, lemon sole, grey sole, or flounder. It's a very simple dish and tastes so light and perfect.

¼ CUP ALL-PURPOSE FLOUR

¼ TEASPOON KOSHER SALT

¼ TEASPOON FRESHLY GROUND BLACK PEPPER

4 SOLE FILLETS (ABOUT 4 OUNCES EACH)

4 TABLESPOONS (½ STICK) UNSALTED BUTTER

2 TEASPOONS FRESH LEMON JUICE

1 TABLESPOON MINCED FLAT-LEAF PARSLEY

Combine flour, salt, and pepper. Dredge each fish fillet in the flour mixture until well coated.

In a large skillet over medium heat, melt 1 tablespoon of the butter. Add the fish and brown about 3 minutes on each side, depending on thickness. Transfer the fish to a platter and tent with foil. Add the remaining butter to pan and turn up the heat to medium-high. When the butter starts to brown, about 3 minutes, add the lemon juice and parsley. Pour the butter over the fish and serve immediately.

2 SERVINGS
PREP TIME: 10 MINUTES
COOK TIME: 10 MINUTES

herb-roasted potatoes

I like to keep things simple for a romantic dinner so that I'm not spending too much time in the kitchen. These potatoes are very easy and taste great.

1 POUND RED-SKINNED POTATOES (CUT IN HALF OR QUARTERED, DEPENDING ON SIZE)

2 TABLESPOONS EXTRA VIRGIN OLIVE OIL

2 TABLESPOONS CHOPPED MIXED FRESH HERBS (SUCH AS ROSEMARY, THYME, PARSLEY, AND CHERVIL)

½ TEASPOON KOSHER SALT

½ TEASPOON FRESHLY GROUND BLACK PEPPER

Preheat the oven to 400°F.

In a large bowl, combine the potatoes, oil, herbs, salt, and pepper. Toss to coat. Place the potatoes on a baking sheet in an even single layer. Roast until fork tender and golden brown, 25 to 30 minutes.

2 SERVINGS
PREP TIME: 10 MINUTES
COOK TIME: 30 MINUTES

haricots verts with grape tomatoes

Haricot vert is French for green bean. I blanch the beans before quickly sautéing them to retain their bright green color. They look beautiful on the plate with the red tomatoes.

Prepare an ice-water bath. Bring a large pot of salted water to a boil over high heat. Add the beans and cook 2 minutes. Drain the beans and plunge into ice water to stop the cooking. Drain.

In a large skillet, melt the butter on medium heat. Add the minced shallots and sauté until tender, about 3 minutes. Add the tomatoes and cook 2 minutes. Add the beans, lemon zest, salt, and pepper. Cook until the beans are heated through, about 5 minutes.

2 SERVINGS
PREP TIME: 10 MINUTES
COOK TIME: 12 MINUTES

$3/4$ POUND HARICOTS VERTS (GREEN BEANS), TRIMMED

1 TABLESPOON UNSALTED BUTTER

1 SHALLOT, MINCED

$1/2$ CUP GRAPE TOMATOES

1 TEASPOON FRESHLY GRATED LEMON ZEST

$1/4$ TEASPOON KOSHER SALT

$1/4$ TEASPOON FRESHLY GROUND BLACK PEPPER

rich chocolate pudding and amaretto whipped cream parfaits

Assemble these parfaits well before dinner and refrigerate until time to serve. Individual desserts like these make your dining companion feel special. The chocolate is so rich and the hint of amaretto in the whipped cream will really set the mood!

FOR THE PUDDING

In a medium saucepan over medium heat, combine the sugar, flour, cocoa, and salt. Mix well. Whisk in the milk. Stir constantly with a wooden spoon while the mixture comes to a low boil and becomes thick, 5 to 7 minutes. Reduce the heat to very low. Stir a couple of tablespoons of the hot mixture into the egg yolks. Stir the egg yolks back into the hot milk mixture. Stir constantly until thickened, 3 to 4 minutes. Remove from the heat and stir in the vanilla. Cover with plastic wrap to prevent skin from forming and let cool completely.

FOR THE WHIPPED CREAM

Using an electric mixer on high speed, beat the cream, sugar, vanilla, and amaretto until stiff peaks form.

TO ASSEMBLE THE PARFAITS

Place one quarter of the pudding in each parfait glass and top each with one quarter of the whipped cream. Sprinkle each with one quarter of the crushed cookies. Repeat layers. Refrigerate, covered, until serving time.

For the pudding

1/2 CUP SUGAR

1/4 CUP ALL-PURPOSE FLOUR

1/2 CUP HIGH-QUALITY DARK COCOA POWDER

1/4 TEASPOON KOSHER SALT

2 CUPS WHOLE MILK

2 LARGE EGG YOLKS, LIGHTLY BEATEN

1 TEASPOON VANILLA EXTRACT

For the whipped cream

1 CUP HEAVY CREAM

1/4 CUP SUGAR

1/2 TEASPOON VANILLA EXTRACT

1 TABLESPOON AMARETTO

6 CHOCOLATE WAFER COOKIES, CRUSHED

2 SERVINGS
PREP TIME: 10 MINUTES
INACTIVE PREP TIME: 2 HOURS
COOK TIME: 11 MINUTES

chocolate royale

A Kir Royale (Champagne with a touch of cassis) is one of my all-time favorite cocktails. A few years ago, I was working with Godiva to develop recipes using their chocolate liqueurs. I decided to try substituting chocolate for cassis and was really surprised by how much I liked it. The chocolate is not over-powering and can be served before dinner as an aperitif or after dinner with dessert.

2 OUNCES GODIVA ORIGINAL
   CHOCOLATE LIQUEUR

6 OUNCES CHAMPAGNE

2 CHOCOLATE-COVERED
   STRAWBERRIES

Pour 1 ounce of chocolate liqueur into each champagne glass and top each with 3 ounces of Champagne. Do not stir. Garnish with a chocolate-covered strawberry.

2 COCKTAILS
PREP TIME: 2 MINUTES

TIP

Flavored whipped creams are an easy way to add a special touch. Simply add your favorite liqueur or extract.

spa lunch

A few years ago, my friend Wendi started a "girls trip" tradition. We like to pick somewhere relaxing with a spa-like atmosphere. One year we went to the Golden Door spa in California and had super healthy food and exercised about four hours a day. Our friend Kelly had a family member who lived nearby drop off a basket of oranges at the front desk—the bottom of the basket was lined with chocolate bars! Needless to say, I didn't lose any weight on that trip.

On another trip, we went to the Caribbean for a week. Our friend Kathy Freston, who is a bestselling author of many books on spirituality and healthy living, guided us in daily meditation. Kathy is a vegan and we ate vegetarian the whole time. It was really a week to cleanse from the inside out.

Sometimes I need an escape but I don't have the time to take a week off to rejuvenate, so I like to have the girls over for a mini spa day at home. I cook an all-vegetarian menu, which is much more exciting than it may sound. My friend Gretta Monahan owns several spas and salons and she shared all of her secret recipes with me, so I make homemade masks and scrubs with ingredients right out of the pantry. I have a great dressing room, so I serve all of the food and drinks in there and set up the spa in my bathroom.

Having a spa day at home is relaxing, fun, and certainly more affordable.

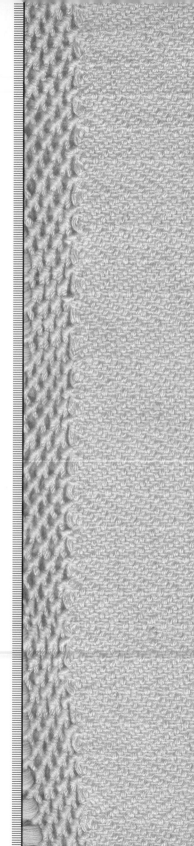

MENU

BEET TARTARE

GRILLED VEGETABLE TOSTADAS

WHEATBERRY SALAD

BROILED SPICY TOFU

MOROCCAN MINT TEA

HEALTHY CARROT CAKE CUPCAKES
WITH CREAM CHEESE FROSTING

SERVES 6

PLAYLIST

*Hôtel Costes Vol. 8 & 9
by Stéphane Pompougnac*

TIP

Make party favors
for your guests by
packaging Epson salts
infused with a few drops
of essential oil.

beet tartare

Beets are full of vitamin C and potassium. This beet tartare is a vegetarian play on traditional steak or tuna tartares. I like to serve it on toasted bread, in endive leaves, or in appetizer spoons.

Preheat oven to 350°F.

Place the beets on a baking sheet and toss with 1 teaspoon of the olive oil. Roast until fork tender, 1 to 1½ hours. Remove and let cool completely. Peel and cut in fine dice.

In a medium bowl, combine the shallots, 2 tablespoons olive oil, the lemon juice, mustard, parsley, tarragon, salt, and pepper. Mix until well combined. Stir in the beets.

6 SERVINGS (ABOUT 1 CUP)
PREP TIME: 10 MINUTES
INACTIVE PREP TIME: 20 MINUTES TO COOL
COOK TIME: 1 TO 1½ HOURS

4 SMALL BEETS, TRIMMED

2 TABLESPOONS PLUS 1 TEASPOON EXTRA VIRGIN OLIVE OIL

¼ CUP MINCED SHALLOTS

1 TABLESPOON FRESH LEMON JUICE

1 TABLESPOON DIJON MUSTARD

1 TABLESPOON MINCED FLAT-LEAF PARSLEY

1 TABLESPOON MINCED TARRAGON

½ TEASPOON KOSHER SALT

PINCH OF FRESHLY GROUND BLACK PEPPER

TOASTED BREAD OR ENDIVE LEAVES, FOR SERVING (OPTIONAL)

grilled vegetable tostadas

These tostadas are really tasty and really healthy. With lots of veggies, protein from the beans, and whole-wheat tortillas, Mom would approve!

For the vegetables

1/4 CUP EXTRA VIRGIN OLIVE OIL

JUICE OF 2 LEMONS

1 TABLESPOON WORCESTERSHIRE SAUCE

1 TEASPOON FRESH THYME LEAVES

1/4 TEASPOON GARLIC POWDER

1/4 TEASPOON ONION POWDER

3/4 TEASPOON KOSHER SALT

1/4 TEASPOON FRESHLY GROUND BLACK PEPPER

2 SMALL ZUCCHINI, THINLY SLICED LENGTHWISE

2 SMALL JAPANESE EGGPLANTS, THINLY SLICED LENGTHWISE

1 SMALL YELLOW SQUASH, THINLY SLICED LENGTHWISE

2 PORTOBELLO MUSHROOM CAPS, THINLY SLICED ON THE DIAGONAL

For the tostadas

3 TABLESPOONS EXTRA VIRGIN OLIVE OIL

1 TABLESPOON FRESH LIME JUICE

1/2 TEASPOON KOSHER SALT

1/4 TEASPOON FRESHLY GROUND BLACK PEPPER

4 CUPS CHOPPED ROMAINE LETTUCE

FOUR 8-INCH FLOUR TORTILLAS (TACO SIZE)

1 CUP REFRIED BEANS

1 AVOCADO, SLICED

6 SERVINGS

PREP TIME: 20 MINUTES

INACTIVE PREP TIME: 3 HOURS AND UP TO OVERNIGHT

COOK TIME: 25 MINUTES

FOR THE VEGETABLES

In a small bowl, combine the olive oil, lemon juice, Worcestershire, thyme, garlic powder, onion powder, salt, and pepper. Whisk until emulsified.

Place the zucchini, eggplant, squash, and mushrooms in a sealable container or resealable plastic bag. Pour the marinade over the vegetables and toss to combine. Refrigerate at least 3 hours and up to overnight, tossing vegetables once or twice.

FOR THE TOSTADAS

Preheat oven to 250°F.

In a large bowl, whisk the olive oil and lime juice. Season with the salt and pepper. Toss with the romaine.

Heat a grill pan over medium heat. Spray each tortilla with nonstick cooking spray on both sides. Cook on the grill pan about 2 minutes per side. Spread with refried beans. Place on a baking sheet in the oven to keep warm.

Remove the vegetables from the marinade and grill for 3 to 4 minutes. Top each tortilla with vegetables, lettuce, and avocado slices.

Cut the tostadas into quarters and place on a serving platter.

wheatberry salad

Wheatberries are a whole grain and therefore high in fiber. I love their nutty flavor combined with the tart Granny Smith apples and cranberries. The chickpeas and pecans add some protein, too!

Combine the wheatberries, water, and 1 teaspoon salt in a medium saucepan. Bring to a boil. Reduce the heat to a simmer and partially cover. Cook 1 hour, until tender. Drain and let cool.

In a large bowl, combine cooked wheatberries with the chickpeas, apple, cranberries, pecans, chives, olive oil, lemon juice, salt, and pepper. Toss to combine.

6 SERVINGS (ABOUT 7 CUPS)
PREP TIME: 15 MINUTES
INACTIVE PREP TIME: 30 MINUTES TO COOL
  THE WHEATBERRIES
COOK TIME: 1 HOUR

$1\frac{1}{2}$ CUPS WHEATBERRIES

4 CUPS WATER

1 TEASPOON KOSHER SALT

ONE 14-OUNCE CAN CHICKPEAS, DRAINED AND RINSED

1 GRANNY SMITH APPLE, CORED AND DICED

$\frac{1}{3}$ CUP DRIED CRANBERRIES

$\frac{1}{3}$ CUP CHOPPED PECANS

2 TABLESPOONS MINCED CHIVES

$\frac{1}{4}$ CUP EXTRA VIRGIN OLIVE OIL

2 TABLESPOONS FRESH LEMON JUICE

1 TEASPOON KOSHER SALT

$\frac{1}{4}$ TEASPOON FRESHLY GROUND BLACK PEPPER

TIP

Look for wheatberries in the bulk foods section of the grocery store.

broiled spicy tofu

Don't turn your nose up at tofu! An excellent source of soy protein and so versatile, tofu takes on any flavor that you want it to. It's so easy . . . marinate and stick it under the broiler. That's it!

TWO 14-OUNCE PACKAGES EXTRA FIRM TOFU

$\frac{1}{2}$ CUP BBQ SAUCE, STORE-BOUGHT OR HOMEMADE (PAGE 245)

1 TABLESPOON FRESH LEMON JUICE

2 TEASPOONS SRIRACHA HOT SAUCE

Drain the tofu. Line a colander with paper towels and place tofu on top. Cover the tofu with more paper towels and place something heavy on top, like a small skillet or heavy plate. Allow the tofu to sit at least 30 minutes. Remove and slice into ½-inch-thick pieces.

In a shallow baking dish, combine the BBQ sauce, lemon juice, and hot sauce. Add the tofu and toss to cover in sauce. Let marinate in the refrigerator at least 1 hour.

Take the tofu out of the refrigerator 20 minutes before cooking.

Preheat the broiler. Place the tofu in a broiler-proof pan and place under the broiler for about 7 minutes, until the tofu is heated through and beginning to brown on the top.

6 SERVINGS (ABOUT 16 PIECES)
PREP TIME: 15 MINUTES
INACTIVE PREP TIME: 30 MINUTES TO DRAIN TOFU, 1 HOUR TO MARINATE, 20 MINUTES TO BRING TO ROOM TEMPERATURE.
COOK TIME: ABOUT 7 MINUTES

moroccan mint tea

When I was in Israel we drank this tea every night after dinner. The mint is calming and refreshing. If you can find agave nectar, try it. I really like the way it tastes, and it has a very low glycemic index, which means it doesn't cause a sharp rise or fall in blood sugar.

Bring the water to a boil. Put the mint leaves, tea bags, and agave nectar into a teapot. Pour in the water and let steep 5 minutes. Strain and serve.

6 SERVINGS
PREP TIME: 2 MINUTES
INACTIVE PREP TIME: 5 MINUTES
COOK TIME: 5 MINUTES

6 CUPS WATER

2 CUPS MINT LEAVES, LIGHTLY PACKED

2 GREEN TEA BAGS

$\frac{1}{4}$ CUP AGAVE NECTAR OR HONEY

healthy carrot cake cupcakes with cream cheese frosting

The words "healthy" and "dessert" don't usually go in the same sentence. At least in my books, anyway. The exception to the rule? These delectable carrot cake cupcakes! With a pound of carrots and whole-wheat flour, they are so yummy *and* guilt-free!

For the cupcakes

2 CUPS WHOLE-WHEAT PASTRY
  FLOUR

1 CUP ALL-PURPOSE FLOUR

2 TEASPOONS BAKING SODA

1½ TEASPOONS GROUND CINNAMON

1 TEASPOON GROUND GINGER

½ TEASPOON GROUND NUTMEG

½ TEASPOON KOSHER SALT

1 CUP LIGHTLY PACKED BROWN
  SUGAR

¼ CUP CANOLA OIL

2 EXTRA LARGE EGGS

½ CUP PLAIN YOGURT

1 POUND CARROTS, GRATED (ABOUT
  4 CUPS)

⅓ CUP GOLDEN RAISINS

For the frosting

4 OUNCES LIGHT CREAM CHEESE
  (I USE NEUFCHÂTEL), AT ROOM
  TEMPERATURE

1 CUP CONFECTIONERS' SUGAR

¼ CUP FINELY CHOPPED WALNUTS

FOR THE CUPCAKES

Preheat oven to 350°F. Line a muffin tin with paper liners.

In a medium bowl, sift together the flours, baking soda, cinnamon, ginger, nutmeg, and salt. Set aside. With an electric mixer, beat the brown sugar and oil for about 5 minutes. Add the eggs, one at a time. Stir in the yogurt, carrots, and raisins. Mix in the flour mixture until just combined.

Using a 3-ounce ice-cream scoop or a ⅓ cup measure, spoon batter into paper-lined muffin tins. Bake for 20 minutes or until a toothpick comes out clean. Let cool completely on a wire rack.

FOR THE FROSTING

Using an electric mixer, whip cream cheese and confectioners' sugar. Spread each cupcake with cream cheese frosting and sprinkle with walnuts. Store in an airtight container.

12 CUPCAKES
PREP TIME: 20 MINUTES
INACTIVE PREP TIME: 30 MINUTES TO COOL
  THE CUPCAKES
COOK TIME: 20 MINUTES

Spa Recipes, Courtesy of Gretta Monahan

SPA MENU

HONEY-OATMEAL FACIAL

STRAWBERRY HAND AND FOOT SCRUB

CUCUMBER COOLING MASK

OATMEAL, ALMOND, AND AVOCADO BODY SCRUB

ROSE PETAL STEAM

SHINY HAIR RINSE

FROM THE PANTRY

- ALMONDS: act as an emollient and skin softener
- APPLE CIDER VINEGAR: rich in alpha-hydroxy acids, and gives softer, smoother skin and scalp
- AVOCADO: contains collagen-building properties that help with fine lines and wrinkles, and helps repair rough, dry skin
- CUCUMBER: acts as a cooling agent, and reduces eye puffiness
- HONEY: rejuvenates and nourishes skin and fights fine lines and wrinkles
- OATMEAL: anti-inflammatory and anti-itch, acts as a skin soother
- STRAWBERRIES: skin soother, and packed with antioxidants
- PLAIN YOGURT: a natural moisturizer

EQUIPMENT

- BLENDER
- TEA KETTLE
- GLASS BOWLS
- MEASURING CUPS
- TOWELS

TIPS

- Stainless steel, enamel, and glass are the best materials to use.
- Avoid use of reactive metals such as silver, copper, aluminum, Teflon, or cast iron.
- Start your spa experience with a shower to remove any lotions, perfumes, and surface dirt.
- Have plenty of extra towels on hand.
- Buy inexpensive house slippers for each guest to wear and that can be worn during the spa experience and taken home as a party favor.

honey-oatmeal facial

1/4 CUP OATMEAL
1 TABLESPOON HONEY
3 TABLESPOONS PLAIN YOGURT

Finely grind the oatmeal in a blender or food processor. In a small bowl, combine the honey and yogurt. Stir in the oatmeal and mix well. Smooth over face and neck. Let sit 10 to 15 minutes. Rinse with warm water. Follow with moisturizer.

strawberry hand and foot scrub

1 CUP STRAWBERRIES
1/4 CUP COARSE SEA SALT
1/4 CUP SHOWER GEL

Puree all ingredients in a blender or food processor. Over a large bowl or bath tub, massage into hands and feet. Let sit 10 to 15 minutes. Rinse and pat dry. Follow with moisturizer.

cucumber cooling mask

1 TABLESPOON WITCH HAZEL

1/2 CUCUMBER, CHOPPED

1/4 CUP ALOE VERA GEL

1 TABLESPOON CORNSTARCH

2 CUCUMBER SLICES

Mix witch hazel, chopped cucumber, and aloe vera in a blender or food processor. Add cornstarch to thicken. Chill in refrigerator for 1 hour. Smooth over face and neck and place cucumber slices over eyes. Let sit 10 to 15 minutes. Rinse and pat dry. Follow with moisturizer.

oatmeal, almond, and avocado body scrub

1/2 CUP ALMONDS

1 CUP OATMEAL

1 RIPE AVOCADO, PITTED, PEELED, AND DICED

1/4 CUP PLAIN YOGURT

Combine all ingredient in a blender or food processor. Rub mixture all over body. Rinse thoroughly and pat dry. Follow with body lotion.

rose petal steam

1 CUP FRESH ROSE PETALS (BE SURE THEY ARE CHEMICAL FREE)

1 GALLON NEAR-BOILING WATER

Place rose petals in a large bowl and add the water. Lean over the bowl and cover head with a towel to keep steam in. Follow with moisturizer. Face should be 10 to 12 inches from the bowl. Steam for 10 minutes. Follow with moisturizer.

shiny hair rinse

1/2 CUP APPLE CIDER VINEGAR

1 QUART WATER

Combine vinegar and water in a pitcher or jar. Shampoo and rinse. Pour mixture onto hair, massaging into hair and scalp. Rinse thoroughly and condition as usual.

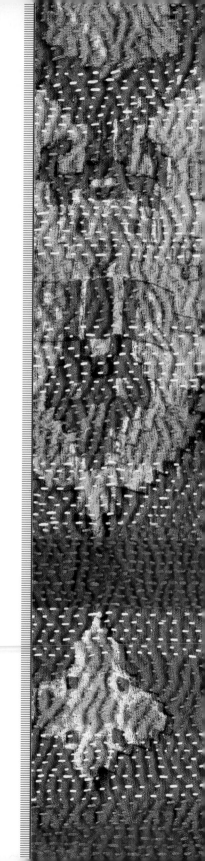

cinco de mayo celebration

A couple of years ago, I took a trip to Mexico City. I loved the culture, the people, the outdoor markets, and especially the food. I ate everything that wasn't nailed down, from the top restaurants like Aguila y Sol and Izote, to the *tortas* made by street vendors. I tried it all, except for the fried grasshoppers. My friend Ahmad loved them, saying they were crunchy and salty, but I wasn't as adventuresome.

I will take any excuse to make guacamole and Margaritas and here you will find my annual Cinco de Mayo fiesta menu. I play Latin music and decorate with bright colors. But I also make this meal anytime I get a craving for Mexican.

MENU

ROASTED GARLIC GUACAMOLE

BLACK BEANS

RED SNAPPER VERACRUZANA

CILANTRO-LIME RICE

PINEAPPLE-COCONUT SUNDAES

PINK GRAPEFRUIT MARGARITAS

SERVES 6 TO 8

WINE

Sauvignon Blanc
Pouilly - Fuissé

PLAYLIST

"T Chintchinote" • BY CÉSARIA ÉVORA
"Cade Voce" • BY SABRINA MALHEIROS
"Me Laman Calle" • BY MANU CHAO
"Contigo" • BY FEDERICO AUBELE
"Canto de Ossanha" • BY PAULA MORELENBAUM

roasted garlic guacamole

My number one weakness is guacamole with tortilla chips. I cannot get enough of it. I usually double this recipe because by the time my guests arrive, half of the guacamole has mysteriously disappeared. One afternoon I tried roasting the garlic before adding it to the avocado and I loved the effect. The garlic is much milder and sweeter and tastes great with the spicy serrano pepper.

1 HEAD GARLIC

1 TEASPOON OLIVE OIL

½ SERRANO PEPPER

4 HASS AVOCADOES, HALVED, PITTED, AND PEELED

JUICE OF 1 LIME

1½ TEASPOONS KOSHER SALT

1 TEASPOON FRESHLY GROUND BLACK PEPPER

½ CUP CHOPPED CILANTRO

TORTILLA CHIPS, FOR SERVING

Preheat the oven to 400°F. Slice the top off the head of garlic. Place the garlic on a sheet of aluminum foil and drizzle with the olive oil. Wrap the garlic tightly. Roast for about 30 minutes, depending on the size of the garlic, until soft and golden brown. Let cool completely. Squeeze the peel of each clove to release the garlic.

In a food processor, combine the garlic, serrano, avocados, lime juice, salt, and pepper. Pulse until chunky. Transfer to a bowl and stir in cilantro. Serve with tortilla chips.

6 TO 8 SERVINGS (ABOUT 4 CUPS)
PREP TIME: 15 MINUTES
INACTIVE PREP TIME: 45 MINUTES TO COOL GARLIC
COOK TIME: 30 MINUTES

black beans

I can't have Mexican food without beans and rice. These black beans are very simple and quick to prepare because I use canned beans. The sautéed onions and peppers combined with the spices and tomatoes add plenty of flavor—and only take about 30 minutes to cook.

Heat the olive oil in a large skillet over medium heat. Add the onion and green bell pepper. Sauté until the onions are translucent, about 5 minutes. Stir in the chili powder, cumin, coriander, and bay leaf. Cook 2 to 3 minutes. Add the black beans, tomatoes, salt, pepper, and water. Bring to a low boil. Reduce heat to a simmer and cook 30 minutes. Remove the bay leaf before serving.

6 TO 8 SERVINGS
PREP TIME: 10 MINUTES
COOK TIME: 40 MINUTES

1 TABLESPOON OLIVE OIL

1 YELLOW ONION, DICED

1 GREEN BELL PEPPER, DICED

1 TABLESPOON CHILI POWDER

1 TEASPOON GROUND CUMIN

1 TEASPOON GROUND CORIANDER

1 BAY LEAF

TWO 14-OUNCE CANS BLACK BEANS, RINSED AND DRAINED

ONE 14-OUNCE CAN DICED TOMATOES, DRAINED

1 TEASPOON KOSHER SALT

$\frac{1}{2}$ TEASPOON FRESHLY GROUND BLACK PEPPER

1 CUP WATER

red snapper veracruzana

This is a traditional dish from the region of Veracruz in Mexico. Oftentimes when we think of Mexican food, we just envision burritos and lots of melted cheese, but the cuisine has so much more to offer. When I returned from a trip to Mexico City a few years ago, I had a Mexican dinner party and this turned out to be one of the easiest dishes I've ever made for entertaining.

¼ CUP OLIVE OIL

2 LARGE YELLOW ONIONS, FINELY CHOPPED

6 GARLIC CLOVES, MINCED

3 JALAPEÑOS, SEEDED AND MINCED

½ CUP DRY WHITE WINE

ONE 28-OUNCE CAN DICED TOMATOES, WITH JUICES

1 TABLESPOON SUGAR

¼ CUP MINCED FLAT-LEAF PARSLEY

2 TABLESPOONS DRAINED CAPERS

1 CUP LARGE GREEN OLIVES, PITS REMOVED AND COARSELY CHOPPED

2 BAY LEAVES

KOSHER SALT AND FRESHLY GROUND BLACK PEPPER

EIGHT 4-OUNCE RED SNAPPER FILLETS

KOSHER SALT AND FRESHLY GROUND BLACK PEPPER

CILANTRO SPRIGS AND LIME WEDGES, FOR GARNISH

Heat the olive oil in a large skillet over medium heat. Add the onions, garlic, and jalapeños. Sauté until the onions are soft, about 10 minutes. Add the white wine and use a wooden spoon to scrape up any brown bits from the bottom of the pan. Stir in tomatoes, sugar, parsley, capers, olives, bay leaves, 1 teaspoon salt, and ½ teaspoon pepper. Reduce the heat to low, cover, and simmer for 15 minutes.

Season each side of the fish with salt and pepper. Place each fillet on the sauce and use a spoon to cover the fish with sauce. Cover and cook for 8 to 10 minutes, until the fish is opaque. Place the fish on a serving platter and spoon sauce over each fillet. Remove the bay leaves. Serve garnished with cilantro and lime wedges.

6 TO 8 SERVINGS
PREP TIME: 15 MINUTES
COOK TIME: 35 MINUTES

cilantro-lime rice

This rice is so refreshing, especially next to the bold tastes of the rest of the meal. The lime juice brightens up the flavors of everything on the plate and the cilantro adds a nice color.

Bring the water, lime juice, and salt to a boil. Add the rice and return to a boil for 2 to 3 minutes. Reduce the heat to a simmer, cover, and cook for about 20 minutes, until all the water is absorbed. Turn off the heat and allow the rice to steam, covered, for 5 minutes. Fluff the rice with a fork and stir in the cilantro.

4 CUPS WATER

JUICE OF 1 LIME

2 TEASPOONS KOSHER SALT

2 CUPS LONG-GRAIN WHITE RICE

¾ CUP CHOPPED CILANTRO

6 TO 8 SERVINGS
PREP TIME: 5 MINUTES
INACTIVE PREP TIME: 5 MINUTES
COOK TIME: 25 MINUTES

pineapple-coconut sundaes

My recipe tester, Katrina Norwood, told me that she made these on a cold day and was instantly transported to Mexico—just what I like to hear! These are really easy to assemble. By lightly grilling the pineapple, all the sugars come out and caramelize. If you can't find coconut ice cream, sorbet tastes just as good.

1 PINEAPPLE, PEELED, CORED AND CUT INTO 8 RINGS

ABOUT 1 QUART COCONUT ICE CREAM

ABOUT 1 CUP CARAMEL SAUCE

8 SPRIGS FRESH MINT

Heat a grill pan over medium-high heat. Coat with nonstick cooking spray. Grill the pineapple slices for 2 to 3 minutes on each side.

Place each slice of pineapple in an individual serving bowl. Top with a scoop of coconut ice cream and drizzle with caramel sauce. Garnish with mint.

8 SERVINGS
PREP TIME: 10 MINUTES
COOK TIME: 6 MINUTES

pink grapefruit margaritas

Nothing gets a party started like Margaritas! Make a pitcher of these and your guests are sure to get talking. These call for ruby red grapefruit juice instead of lime juice to change things up a bit—and the pale pink color is so pretty garnished with a wedge of lime.

Rub the outside rim of each margarita glass with one of the lime wedges. Press the top of each glass in the kosher salt to coat the rim.

Combine the grapefruit juice, sugar, triple sec, and tequila in a pitcher. Stir until the sugar dissolves. Serve on the rocks, or blend with ice for frozen. Garnish with a lime wedge.

6 TO 8 SERVINGS (ABOUT 40 OUNCES)
PREP TIME: 10 MINUTES

2 LIMES, CUT INTO WEDGES

KOSHER SALT, IN A SHALLOW DISH, FOR RIMMING THE GLASSES

1 CUP RUBY RED GRAPEFRUIT JUICE (FRESH OR STORE-BOUGHT)

1 TABLESPOON SUPERFINE SUGAR

2 CUPS TRIPLE SEC

2 CUPS GOOD-QUALITY SILVER TEQUILA

ICE

mother's day brunch

When I was growing up, Mom was my hero. She had the answers to all my questions, knew just the right thing to say when I was sad, and always encouraged me to be my best. I wanted to be just like her.

In our house, we had a tradition of Mother's Day breakfast-in-bed. She'd play along, pretending to sleep in as I banged pots and pans in the kitchen, usually generating such a mess that it was more work for her to clean up than the relaxation she gained from a leisurely morning in bed. The menu varied from year to year—I made everything from pancakes to biscuits to beignets. The food was far from perfect, but she acted as if it were a fine dining experience.

These days, I like to invite Mom for a Mother's Day brunch with family and invite friends to join as well. It's a great time of year to hit up the farmers' market and pick up spring fruits and vegetables to make a beautiful spread in honor of the most important woman in my life. Love you, Mom!

MENU

SMOKED SALMON CANAPÉS
WITH DIJON CRÈME FRAÎCHE

MINTED PEA SOUP

ASPARAGUS AND SPINACH FRITTATA

BLUEBERRY SOUR CREAM COFFEE CAKE
WITH LEMON GLAZE

POMEGRANATE ELDERFLOWER
CHAMPAGNE COCKTAIL

SERVES 6

WINE

Sancerre
fruity Chardonnay

PLAYLIST

"Tea for Two"
BY SARAH VAUGHN (CHRIS SHAW REMIX)

"Cruisin'"
PERFORMED BY GWYNETH PALTROW AND HUEY LEWIS

"Just the Way You Are"
PERFORMED BY MAGGIE GYLLENHALL

"These Are the Days" • BY JAMIE CULLUM

"Don't Know Why" • BY NORAH JONES

smoked salmon canapés with dijon crème fraîche

These little smoked salmon canapés with Dijon crème fraîche look so elegant yet take no time at all to whip up. They are perfect for brunch, but also great with afternoon tea or for cocktail hour.

In a small bowl, combine the crème fraîche, mustard, honey, lemon juice, and minced dill. Chill at least 4 hours, until serving time.

Cut the crusts from the pumpernickel. Use the cookie cutter to cut bread into circles. Lightly toast. Let cool.

Spread the Dijon mixture on the pumpernickel rounds. Top with a piece of salmon and garnish with dill.

6 SERVINGS (ABOUT 50 PIECES)
PREP TIME: 20 MINUTES
INACTIVE PREP TIME: 4 HOURS TO CHILL
  SAUCE
COOK TIME: 10 MINUTES TO TOAST BREAD

3 TABLESPOONS CRÈME FRAÎCHE

2 TABLESPOONS DIJON MUSTARD

1 TABLESPOON HONEY

1 TABLESPOON FRESH LEMON JUICE

1 TABLESPOON FRESH MINCED DILL

6 LARGE SLICES PUMPERNICKEL
  BREAD

$\frac{1}{2}$ POUND THINLY SLICED SMOKED
  SALMON

MINCED DILL FOR GARNISH

SPECIAL EQUIPMENT: $1\frac{1}{2}$-INCH ROUND
  COOKIE CUTTER

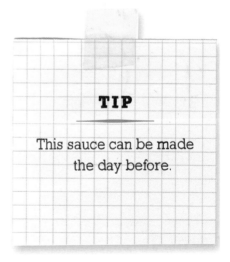

TIP

This sauce can be made the day before.

minted pea soup

This classic soup is one of my favorites. Use fresh peas if you can find them or substitute with frozen. It really tastes like spring and is delicious served hot or chilled, so take your pick.

2 TABLESPOONS (¼ STICK) UNSALTED BUTTER

1 SMALL SWEET ONION, CHOPPED

TWO 10-OUNCE PACKAGES FROZEN PEAS

1 QUART LOW-SODIUM CHICKEN BROTH

½ CUP MINCED FRESH MINT

1 TEASPOON GRATED LEMON ZEST

1 TEASPOON KOSHER SALT

½ TEASPOON FRESHLY GROUND BLACK PEPPER

½ CUP HEAVY CREAM

PLAIN YOGURT AND MINT LEAVES, FOR GARNISH

In a stockpot over medium heat, melt the butter. Add the onions and sauté until translucent, about 10 minutes. Add the peas, broth, and mint. Bring to a boil, then reduce the heat to a simmer. Cover and cook 20 minutes. Stir in the lemon zest, salt, and pepper, cover, and cook an additional 10 minutes.

Transfer in batches to a blender (or use an immersion blender) and puree until smooth.

Return to the pot and stir in the heavy cream. Cook on low for 10 minutes.

Serve garnished with a dollop of yogurt and a small mint leaf.

6 SERVINGS (ABOUT 6½ CUPS)
PREP TIME: 10 MINUTES
COOK TIME: 50 MINUTES

asparagus and spinach frittata

A frittata is so much easier than making omelets, and it can be served at room temperature. This frittata is so flavorful—it tastes like spring, with the leeks, asparagus, and spinach. I love the creamy goat cheese but you could also substitute feta or any other soft cheese.

2 TABLESPOONS (¼ STICK) UNSALTED BUTTER

2 LEEKS, WHITES ONLY, THINLY SLICED

8 LARGE EGGS, BEATEN

1 CUP BLANCHED ASPARAGUS TIPS

2 CUPS COOKED FRESH OR FROZEN SPINACH, THAWED AND SQUEEZED OF EXCESS WATER

½ CUP FRESH BASIL, CHIFFONADED

4 OUNCES GOAT CHEESE, CRUMBLED

½ CUP GRATED PARMESAN CHEESE

½ TEASPOON KOSHER SALT

¼ TEASPOON FRESHLY GROUND BLACK PEPPER

¼ CUP DRY BREAD CRUMBS

Preheat the oven to 350°F.

In a medium skillet over medium heat, melt the butter. Add the leeks and sauté about 10 minutes. Remove from heat and cool completely.

In a large mixing bowl, combine the eggs with the leeks, asparagus, spinach, basil, goat cheese, Parmesan, salt, and pepper. Mix well.

Spray a 9-inch nonstick cake pan or springform pan with nonstick cooking spray. Add the bread crumbs and shake until the bread crumbs evenly coat the pan. Pour the egg mixture into pan. Bake for 30 to 35 minutes, until solid and a toothpick comes out clean. Cool in the pan over a wire rack for 5 minutes. Invert the frittata onto a plate, then flip right side up onto a serving plate or remove sides of springform pan and transfer to a serving plate. Can be served warm or at room temperature.

6 SERVINGS
PREP TIME: 20 MINUTES
INACTIVE PREP TIME: 5 MINUTES
COOK TIME: 45 MINUTES

blueberry sour cream coffee cake with lemon glaze

Sometimes I think I love brunch only because it's an excuse to make this coffee cake. Once I accidentally bought whole-wheat cake flour and made it with that and it was actually really good, just a little denser in texture. Try it with regular cake flour, or whole-wheat for a healthier take.

For the topping

6 TABLESPOONS (¾ STICK) UNSALTED BUTTER, MELTED

¾ CUP LIGHT BROWN SUGAR

1 CUP FINELY CHOPPED WALNUTS

1 TABLESPOON GROUND CINNAMON

2 TABLESPOONS ALL-PURPOSE FLOUR

For the batter

3 CUPS CAKE FLOUR

2 TEASPOONS BAKING POWDER

1 TEASPOON BAKING SODA

¾ TEASPOON KOSHER SALT

½ POUND (2 STICKS) UNSALTED BUTTER, AT ROOM TEMPERATURE

2 CUPS WHITE SUGAR

4 EXTRA LARGE EGGS, AT ROOM TEMPERATURE

1 CUP SOUR CREAM

2 TEASPOONS VANILLA EXTRACT

1 CUP BLUEBERRIES

Preheat the oven to 350°F. Grease and flour an 11-inch springform pan.

FOR THE TOPPING

In a bowl, combine the melted butter, brown sugar, walnuts, cinnamon, and flour. Set aside.

FOR THE BATTER

In a mixing bowl, sift the flour with the baking powder, baking soda, and salt. Set aside.

Using an electric mixer, cream the butter and sugar until light and fluffy, about 5 minutes. Add the eggs, one at a time. Mix in the sour cream and vanilla. Slowly add dry ingredients, taking care not to overmix.

Pour one half of batter into the prepared pan. Sprinkle the blueberries evenly over the batter. Pour the remaining batter over the blueberries. Sprinkle with the topping. Bake 50 to 60 minutes. Cool completely on a wire rack and remove from springform pan. Transfer to serving plate and drizzle with glaze.

continued

blueberry sour cream coffee cake with lemon glaze, *continued*

For the glaze

½ CUP CONFECTIONERS' SUGAR

2 TABLESPOONS MILK

1 TABLESPOON FRESH LEMON JUICE

FOR THE GLAZE

Whisk all ingredients together until smooth. Drizzle over the cake.

6 SERVINGS
PREP TIME: 30 MINUTES
COOK TIME: 60 MINUTES

pomegranate elderflower champagne cocktail

I had never had tasted elderflower before I tried St. Germain liqueur, but it's really unique and just lovely—perfect for brunch!

In a champagne glass, combine the elderflower liqueur and pomegranate juice. Top with the Champagne.

1 COCKTAIL
PREP TIME: 2 MINUTES

- 1 OUNCE ST. GERMAIN ELDERFLOWER LIQUEUR
- 1 OUNCE POMEGRANATE JUICE
- 3 OUNCES CHAMPAGNE OR SPARKLING WINE

garden party

There's something that sounds so whimsical about having a garden party. As soon as someone says the words, my mind goes to *Alice in Wonderland* and I start having visions of the Mad Hatter. I set up a table in my garden and decorate with flowers, greens, and herbs, and I serve a variety of mini sandwiches. One of the great things about this party is that it works any time of day—beautiful for brunch, lunch, afternoon, or even dusk.

MENU

CARAMELIZED VIDALIA ONION DIP
WITH HOMEMADE POTATO CHIPS

CURRIED CHICKEN SALAD IN PITAS

TOMATO SANDWICHES

SHRIMP SALAD SANDWICHES

BIBB LETTUCE SALAD WITH AVOCADO,
GRAPEFRUIT, AND TOASTED ALMONDS

PASSION FRUIT MOJITOS

FROZEN LEMON CREAM PIE

SERVES 8

WINE

*Chablis
Sancerre*

PLAYLIST

"Send Someone Away" • BY EMBEE (RADIO)
"Heaven" • BY JOHN LEGEND
"No One" • BY ALICIA KEYS
"Clocks" • BY COLDPLAY (RHYTHMS DEL MUNDO MIX)
"Quando, Quando, Quando" • BY MICHAEL BUBLE,
FEATURING NELLY FURTADO

caramelized vidalia onion dip with homemade potato chips

Onion dip is a total classic. The caramelized Vidalia onions add a whole new element of sweet flavor to the savory dip. I like to make homemade potato chips—they are much easier than one might think. If you're in a time crunch, though, just buy kettle chips from the grocery store.

Heat olive oil in a medium skillet over medium-high heat. Add the onions and sauté 5 to 7 minutes, until beginning to brown. Stir in the water and scrape up any brown bits from the bottom of the pan. Turn the heat to low and cook 30 to 35 minutes, stirring occasionally, until the onions are golden brown. If the pan ever looks too dry, add a tablespoon of water. Let cool completely.

In a medium bowl, combine the cream cheese, mayonnaise, sour cream, Worcestershire, garlic salt, onion powder, and pepper. Using a electric mixer, beat until smooth. Stir in the reserved onions and the scallions.

Chill until serving time.

Serve with chips.

1 TABLESPOON OLIVE OIL

1 LARGE VIDALIA ONION, VERY THINLY SLICED (IF YOU CAN'T FIND VIDALIA, USE ANOTHER SWEET VARIETY LIKE WALLA WALLA, MAUI, OR TEXAS SPRING)

1/4 CUP WATER

ONE 8-OUNCE PACKAGE CREAM CHEESE, AT ROOM TEMPERATURE

1/2 CUP MAYONNAISE

1/4 CUP SOUR CREAM

1 TEASPOON WORCESTERSHIRE SAUCE

1/2 TEASPOON GARLIC SALT

1/2 TEASPOON ONION POWDER

1/2 TEASPOON FRESHLY GROUND BLACK PEPPER

1 SCALLION, GREEN PART ONLY, THINLY SLICED

HOMEMADE POTATO CHIPS (RECIPE FOLLOWS)

8 SERVINGS (ABOUT 2 1/2 CUPS)
PREP TIME: 25 MINUTES
INACTIVE PREP TIME: AT LEAST 30 MINUTES TO CHILL IN REFRIGERATOR
COOK TIME: 30 MINUTES

TIP

Use leftover dip on a roast beef sandwich— so good!

homemade potato chips

2 SMALL BAKING POTATOES
ABOUT 2 QUARTS PEANUT OIL
KOSHER SALT

Use a mandoline to slice the potatoes ⅛-inch thick. Place the potato slices in a large bowl and cover with cold water. Refrigerate 1 hour. Drain and pat very dry with paper towels.

Heat a few inches of peanut oil to 350°F in a Dutch oven. Fry the potatoes in batches of 10 to 12 depending on the size of your pan, until golden brown, about 4 minutes. Drain on paper towels and sprinkle with salt.

8 SERVINGS
PREP TIME: 10 MINUTES
INACTIVE PREP TIME: 1 HOUR
COOK TIME: 20 MINUTES

curried chicken salad in pitas

This salad has great flavor and excellent texture from the tender chicken, creamy dressing, crunchy apples, and chewy raisins. It's delicious in a pita, but also really nice served on a bed of mixed greens. It makes for perfect lunchbox leftovers, too!

FOR THE CHICKEN

Preheat oven to 400°F.

Place the chicken on a baking sheet skin side up, drizzle with olive oil, and season with salt and pepper. Roast until cooked all the way through, about 30 minutes. Cool to the touch. Remove and discard the skin and bones, and cut the chicken into chunks.

FOR THE SALAD

In a large bowl, combine the mayonnaise, yogurt, lemon juice, curry powder, honey, salt, and pepper. Stir until combined. Add the chicken, apples, raisins, and scallions and mix well.

TO SERVE

Spoon the chicken salad into mini pitas and add a leaf of lettuce.

8 SERVINGS
PREP TIME: 15 MINUTES
INACTIVE PREP TIME: 20 MINUTES
COOK TIME: 30 MINUTES

For the chicken salad

4 BONE-IN, SKIN-ON CHICKEN BREAST HALVES

1 TABLESPOON OLIVE OIL

2 TEASPOONS KOSHER SALT

1 TEASPOON FRESHLY GROUND BLACK PEPPER

1/2 CUP MAYONNAISE

1/4 CUP PLAIN YOGURT

2 TABLESPOONS FRESH LEMON JUICE

2 TEASPOONS CURRY POWDER

2 TEASPOONS HONEY

1 TEASPOON KOSHER SALT

3/4 TEASPOON FRESHLY GROUND BLACK PEPPER, TO TASTE

1 GRANNY SMITH APPLE, CORED AND DICED

1/4 CUP GOLDEN RAISINS

2 TABLESPOONS SCALLIONS, THINLY SLICED

For the sandwiches

ABOUT 24 MINI PITAS

ABOUT 1/2 HEAD OF GREEN LEAF LETTUCE

tomato sandwiches

Tomato sandwiches are a Southern classic, usually eaten in the afternoon as a snack with a big glass of iced sweet tea. They are welcome on my table any time of day. So simple and just divine.

Cut the bread into 2-inch rounds using a small biscuit cutter (you should get two rounds per slice of white bread). Spread each round with mayonnaise. Top half of the bread with a slice of tomato and season with salt and pepper. Top with a basil leaf and the remaining bread rounds.

8 SERVINGS
PREP TIME: 10 MINUTES

8 SLICES WHITE BREAD

$\frac{1}{3}$ CUP MAYONNAISE

2 TO 3 ROMA TOMATOES, EACH
    SLICED INTO 8 ROUNDS

KOSHER SALT AND FRESHLY
    GROUND BLACK PEPPER

8 BASIL LEAVES

SPECIAL EQUIPMENT: 2-INCH BISCUIT
    CUTTER

shrimp salad sandwiches

I love, love, love shrimp salad. I keep mine pretty simple, just shrimp, celery, and scallions. There's something so decadent about eating it on brioche buns, which add a nice buttery taste and fluffy texture.

JUICE OF 1 LEMON (ABOUT 2 TABLE-
   SPOONS)

¾ CUP MAYONNAISE

1 TABLESPOON WHITE WINE VINEGAR

1 TEASPOON DIJON MUSTARD

½ TEASPOON SUGAR

½ TEASPOON KOSHER SALT

½ TEASPOON FRESHLY GROUND
   BLACK PEPPER

2 POUNDS COOKED SHRIMP,
   PEELED, TAILS REMOVED, AND
   DICED

2 CELERY STALKS, FINELY DICED

2 SCALLIONS, THINLY SLICED

BRIOCHE BUNS (16 TO 20 MINIS, OR
   4 OR 5 REGULAR SIZE)

In a large bowl, mix the lemon juice, mayonnaise, vinegar, mustard, sugar, salt, and pepper. Stir in the shrimp, celery, and scallions. Serve on mini brioche buns or regular brioche buns cut into quarters.

8 SERVINGS
PREP TIME: 15 MINUTES

bibb lettuce salad with avocado, grapefruit, and toasted almonds

I could eat this entire salad by myself. It is just the right combination of flavors, and the Bibb lettuce is so delicate next to the other elements of the salad. *C'est magnifique!*

Combine the lettuce, avocado, grapefruit, almonds, and chives in a large salad bowl. In a separate bowl, whisk the shallots, vinegar, olive oil, mustard, honey, salt, and pepper until emulsified. Drizzle onto salad and toss to combine. Serve immediately.

8 SERVINGS
PREP TIME: 15 MINUTES

2 HEADS BIBB LETTUCE, TORN INTO BITE-SIZE PIECES

1 AVOCADO, PITTED, PEELED, AND DICED

1 GRAPEFRUIT, PEEL AND PITH REMOVED, CUT INTO SEGMENTS

$\frac{1}{4}$ CUP TOASTED SLICED ALMONDS

2 TABLESPOONS MINCED CHIVES

2 TABLESPOONS MINCED SHALLOTS

2 TABLESPOONS CHAMPAGNE VINEGAR

3 TABLESPOONS EXTRA VIRGIN OLIVE OIL

1 TEASPOON DIJON MUSTARD

1 TEASPOON HONEY

$\frac{3}{4}$ TEASPOON KOSHER SALT

$\frac{1}{4}$ TEASPOON FRESHLY GROUND BLACK PEPPER

passion fruit mojitos

Casa Tua is one of the chicest restaurants in South Beach, decorated in blue and white, with Moroccan lanterns hanging from trees that look as if they've been there since the start of time. When I walk through the gate I feel as though I've been transported to some faraway place. One night my friend ordered this cocktail and it instantly became my favorite. I asked the bartender how he made it and he was kind enough to share the ingredients with me. Fresh passion fruit is expensive and sometimes hard to find, but look in the freezer section of a Latin grocery store and you are sure to find its pulp.

1 TABLESPOON MINCED FRESH MINT

1½ OUNCES PASSION FRUIT PULP

1½ OUNCES WHITE RUM

1 OUNCE SIMPLE SYRUP

¾ OUNCE FRESH LEMON JUICE

SPLASH OF CLUB SODA

Place mint in bottom of a rocks glass and muddle. In a cocktail shaker filled with ice, combine the passion fruit pulp, rum, syrup, and lemon juice. Strain into the glass and top with a splash of club soda.

1 COCKTAIL
PREP TIME: 5 MINUTES

frozen lemon cream pie

This is one of the easiest and tastiest pies I have ever made. If you're not the best baker, just try making this pie and you will fool everyone into thinking you are an award-winning pie maker.

For the crust
2 CUPS FINELY CRUSHED GRAHAM CRACKER CRUMBS

1/3 CUP SUGAR

1/4 TEASPOON KOSHER SALT

8 TABLESPOONS (1 STICK) UNSALTED BUTTER, MELTED

For the filling
ONE 14-OUNCE CAN SWEETENED CONDENSED MILK

4 EXTRA LARGE EGG YOLKS

1/3 CUP SUGAR

2 TABLESPOONS GRATED LEMON ZEST

3/4 CUP FRESH LEMON JUICE

For the topping
WHIPPED CREAM

CANDIED LEMON PEEL

FOR THE CRUST
Preheat oven to 350°F.

In a medium bowl, combine the graham cracker crumbs, sugar, and salt. Stir in the butter. Transfer to a 9-inch tart pan. Evenly press across the bottom and up the sides to make a crust (I use a metal measuring cup to press the crumbs). Bake 12 minutes. Let cool completely.

FOR THE FILLING
In a large bowl, combine the condensed milk, egg yolks, sugar, lemon zest and juice. Whisk until all the ingredients are completely blended. Pour the filling into the cooled crust. Freeze for at least 2 hours.

FOR THE TOPPING
Top with whipped cream and garnish with candied lemon peel

8 SERVINGS
PREP TIME: 30 MINUTES
INACTIVE PREP TIME: 30 MINUTES TO COOL CRUST, 2 HOURS TO FREEZE
COOK TIME: 12 MINUTES

summer barbecue

Summer is easily my favorite time of year. I spend most of my time in the Hamptons and I just love it. Before I moved there, I envisioned the Hamptons as being "Hollywood East" with glitz and glamour and paparazzi, but it's nothing like that. The beaches are some of the most beautiful in the world, farmland stretches for miles, and the hour just before sunset is magical. After busy weeks in the city, the Hamptons are very chill and relaxed. There are many parties and events on the weekends, but instead of getting dressed up and fighting the traffic, I think it's more fun to stay home and have friends over for a barbecue.

I never do anything too fussy in the summer. Instead I opt for easy food that's friendly to both kids and adults. I keep everything really simple. Last year, I had what's become an infamous party: a good old-fashioned kegger! Hamburgers, hot dogs, kegs, and boxed wine. It was without a doubt the best party I've ever had. This summer barbecue menu has a little more class, but it would still go great with a keg!

MENU

FRIED ZUCCHINI CHIPS

LAMB BURGERS WITH OLIVE TAPENADE,
PICKLED ONIONS, AND TZATZIKI

ROASTED PORTOBELLO MUSHROOM
CHEESEBURGERS WITH CARAMELIZED
ONIONS AND PIMENTO AÏOLI

SPINACH AND FETA RICE SALAD

BLACKBERRY-ROSEMARY SPLASH

HONEY-CHERRY YOGURT POPSICLES

SERVES 6

WINE

Beaujolais

PLAYLIST

"7 Days in Sunny June" • BY JAMIROQUAI
"No Substitute Love" • BY ESTELLE
"O-o-h Child," • by Nina Simone (NICKODEMUS REMIX)
"Sweet Child of Mine" • BY BOSSA-N-ROSES
"Turn Your Lights Down" • BY BOB MARLEY, FEATURING
LAURYN HILL

fried zucchini chips

There's a restaurant in East Hampton called Nick and Toni's that serves chips similar to these. It's criminal to eat there and not order the zucchini chips. They serve them piled high on a plate with lemon wedges. I can't get enough of them!

Use a mandoline to slice the zucchini very thin. (They should look like potato chips.) Coat zucchini slices with the egg, then dredge a few at a time in the flour.

In a large Dutch oven over medium-high heat, heat the oil to 375°F. Fry the zucchini in batches until golden brown, about 2 to 3 minutes. Drain on paper towels. Sprinkle with salt and a squeeze of lemon juice. Serve immediately.

6 SERVINGS
PREP TIME: 5 MINUTES
COOK TIME: 10 MINUTES

2 MEDIUM ZUCCHINI

1 LARGE EGG, LIGHTLY BEATEN

1 CUP SELF-RISING FLOUR

VEGETABLE OIL, FOR FRYING

KOSHER SALT AND LEMONS, FOR SERVING

lamb burgers with olive tapenade, pickled onions, and tzatziki

There's nothing like a good burger, and these lamb burgers are incredible! I season the meat with herbs that are often found in Greek cooking, like fresh mint and oregano, and the olive tapenade, pickled onions, and tzatziki add so much flavor. Have plenty of extra napkins around—these are so juicy they can get messy!

For the pickled onions

¾ CUP RED WINE VINEGAR

1 TABLESPOON LIGHT BROWN SUGAR

½ TEASPOON KOSHER SALT

1 TEASPOON BLACK PEPPERCORNS

1 BAY LEAF

1 SMALL RED ONION, THINLY SLICED

For the tzatziki

½ CUP PLAIN GREEK-STYLE YOGURT

2 TABLESPOONS CHOPPED, SEEDED CUCUMBER

1 TEASPOON RED WINE VINEGAR

1 TEASPOON MINCED FRESH MINT

PINCH OF KOSHER SALT

For the lamb burgers

2 POUNDS GROUND LAMB

½ MEDIUM YELLOW ONION, GRATED

2 TABLESPOONS MINCED FRESH MINT

1 TABLESPOON MINCED FRESH OREGANO

1 TEASPOON KOSHER SALT

1 TEASPOON FRESHLY GROUND BLACK PEPPER

1 TEASPOON GARLIC POWDER

6 ONION HAMBURGER BUNS

OLIVE TAPENADE, STORE-BOUGHT OR HOMEMADE, AND BIBB LETTUCE LEAVES, FOR SERVING

FOR THE PICKLED ONIONS

In a small saucepan, combine the vinegar, sugar, salt, peppercorns, and bay leaf and bring to a low boil, stirring until sugar dissolves. Pour over onions and refrigerate at least 3 hours and up to overnight.

FOR THE TZATZIKI

Combine all the ingredients and refrigerate until serving time.

FOR THE LAMB BURGERS

Heat the grill to medium-high.

In a medium bowl, combine the lamb, onion, mint, oregano, salt, pepper, and garlic powder. Divide meat into 6 equal portions and shape into patties. Grill about 5 minutes on each side for medium rare, or to desired doneness.

Spread each bun with olive tapenade and stack with a burger, pickled onions, Bibb lettuce, and tzatziki sauce.

6 SERVINGS
PREP TIME: 25 MINUTES
INACTIVE PREP TIME: AT LEAST 3 HOURS FOR PICKLED ONIONS
COOK TIME: 15 MINUTES

roasted portobello mushroom cheeseburgers with caramelized onions and pimento aïoli

Several of my friends are vegetarians, so I came up with this recipe last summer when I was having a barbecue. They are so good, even carnivores will devour them. If you can find Portuguese muffins, their sweet flavor makes for a delicious bun option.

For the burgers

JUICE OF 1 LEMON (2 TO 3 TABLE-
   SPOONS)

1/4 CUP EXTRA VIRGIN OLIVE OIL

2 TABLESPOONS WORCESTERSHIRE
   SAUCE

2 TEASPOONS FRESH THYME LEAVES

1/4 TEASPOON GARLIC POWDER

6 PORTOBELLO MUSHROOMS, WIPED
   CLEAN AND STEMS REMOVED

KOSHER SALT AND FRESHLY
   GROUND BLACK PEPPER

6 SLICES MUENSTER CHEESE
   (OR SWISS, WHITE CHEDDAR,
   PROVOLONE—YOUR CHOICE)

6 PORTUGUESE MUFFINS OR
   BRIOCHE HAMBURGER BUNS,
   BUTTERED AND TOASTED

1 1/2 CUPS LOOSELY PACKED ARUGULA

For the onions

1 TABLESPOON OLIVE OIL

1 MEDIUM VIDALIA ONION, THINLY
   SLICED

1/4 CUP WATER

KOSHER SALT AND FRESHLY
   GROUND BLACK PEPPER

FOR THE BURGERS

In a shallow baking dish, use a whisk to combine the lemon juice, olive oil, Worcestershire, thyme, and garlic powder. Place mushrooms in the marinade, cover, and refrigerate for at least 1 hour. Turn over the mushrooms, cover again, and refrigerate at least another hour. (Mushrooms can marinate for several hours.)

FOR THE ONIONS

In the meantime, make the onions. In a skillet, heat the olive oil over medium heat. Add the onions and cook about 5 minutes, stirring occasionally. Add the water, cover, and reduce heat to low. Cook 20 to 30 minutes, stirring occasionally, until the onions are golden brown. Remove the pan from the heat. Season the onions with salt and pepper. Set aside.

FOR THE AÏOLI

Combine all ingredients in a small bowl. Refrigerate until serving time.

TO FINISH THE BURGERS

Preheat oven to 450°F.

Remove mushrooms from marinade and season with salt and pepper on both sides. Place the mushrooms on a baking sheet, gill sides up. Bake for 5 minutes. Remove from the oven and arrange cheese and caramelized onions on the gills of each mushroom and bake another 5 minutes, until the cheese is melted and bubbly.

Place 1 mushroom on each muffin and garnish with aïoli and arugula. Serve immediately.

6 SERVINGS

PREP TIME: 30 MINUTES
INACTIVE PREP TIME: AT LEAST 2 HOURS
COOK TIME: 30 MINUTES FOR ONIONS, 10
    MINUTES FOR MUSHROOM BURGERS

For the aïoli
½ CUP MAYONNAISE

2 TABLESPOONS JARRED CHOPPED
    PIMENTOS, DRAINED

1 TABLESPOON RED WINE VINEGAR

1 GARLIC CLOVE, MINCED

1 TABLESPOON MINCED FLAT-LEAF
    PARSLEY

KOSHER SALT AND FRESHLY
    GROUND BLACK PEPPER

spinach and feta rice salad

This simple salad makes for the perfect side dish at a summer barbecue. Since the dressing doesn't contain mayonnaise, there's no need to worry about it spoiling in the heat. Cooking the rice in chicken broth (or vegetable broth for a vegetarian-friendly dish) flavored with Middle Eastern spices adds flavor and complements the spinach and feta beautifully.

For the vinaigrette

3 TABLESPOONS EXTRA VIRGIN OLIVE OIL

1 TABLESPOON RED WINE VINEGAR

1 SHALLOT, MINCED

1 TEASPOON KOSHER SALT

1/2 TEASPOON FRESHLY GROUND BLACK PEPPER

For the salad

1 CUP LOW-SODIUM CHICKEN BROTH

1 CUP WATER

1/4 TEASPOON GARLIC SALT

1/4 TEASPOON GROUND CUMIN

1/4 TEASPOON GROUND TURMERIC

1/4 TEASPOON FRESHLY GROUND BLACK PEPPER

1 BAY LEAF

1 CUP WHITE RICE

1/2 TEASPOON KOSHER SALT

1 CUP THAWED FROZEN CHOPPED SPINACH, SQUEEZED OF EXCESS MOISTURE

1 ROASTED RED PEPPER, CHOPPED

2 TABLESPOONS MINCED FRESH CHIVES

1/2 CUP CRUMBLED FETA CHEESE

FOR THE VINAIGRETTE

Mix olive oil, vinegar, shallot, salt, and pepper until emulsified.

FOR THE SALAD

In a medium saucepan, combine the broth, water, garlic salt, cumin, turmeric, pepper, and bay leaf. Bring to a boil. Stir in the rice and salt, lower the heat to a simmer, and cover. Cook 20 minutes, until liquid is totally absorbed. Fluff rice with a fork. Set aside to cool.

In a large bowl, combine rice with spinach, roasted red pepper, chives, and feta. Stir in the vinaigrette. This can be made in advance.

6 SERVINGS
PREP TIME: 10 MINUTES
INACTIVE PREP TIME: 15 MINUTES FOR RICE TO COOL
COOK TIME: 20 MINUTES

blackberry-rosemary splash

Blackberries and rosemary nicely complement one another in this refreshing summer cocktail. Everyone will be asking you for the recipe.

FOR THE SIMPLE SYRUP

Combine the sugar, water, and rosemary in a small saucepan. Bring to a boil, stirring constantly until sugar dissolves completely. Set aside and let cool to room temperature. Cover and refrigerate. Will keep for up to a week.

FOR THE COCKTAIL

Put the blackberries in a cocktail shaker and crush them lightly. Add ice to fill the shaker, and the vodka, lemon juice, and simple syrup. Shake vigorously. Strain into a martini glass and top with Champagne. Garnish with a rosemary sprig.

1 COCKTAIL
PREP TIME: 3 MINUTES
SYRUP: 10 MINUTES

For the simple syrup
$\frac{1}{2}$ CUP SUGAR
$\frac{1}{2}$ CUP WATER
1 LARGE SPRIG FRESH ROSEMARY

For the cocktail
$\frac{1}{4}$ CUP BLACKBERRIES
2 OUNCES VODKA
1 OUNCE FRESH LEMON JUICE
1 TABLESPOON ROSEMARY SIMPLE SYRUP
2 TO 4 OUNCES CHAMPAGNE OR SPARKLING WINE
ROSEMARY SPRIG, FOR GARNISH

honey-cherry yogurt popsicles

Kids and adults alike will enjoy these pops. The best part? They are guilt free. These will become a staple in your freezer all summer long.

Mix the yogurt and honey until combined. Stir in the cherries. Divide among 6 ice-pop molds. Freeze at least 4 hours, until completely solid.

1 CUP PLAIN GREEK-STYLE YOGURT

½ CUP HONEY

½ CUP COARSELY CHOPPED PITTED CHERRIES (THAWED, IF FROZEN)

6 SERVINGS

PREP TIME: 5 MINUTES

INACTIVE PREP TIME: AT LEAST 4 HOURS TO FREEZE

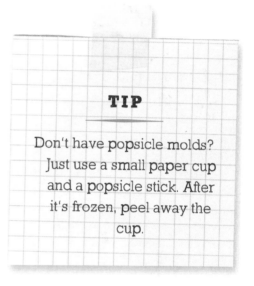

TIP

Don't have popsicle molds? Just use a small paper cup and a popsicle stick. After it's frozen, peel away the cup.

fourth of july celebration

All year long, I look forward to the Fourth of July. I love the all-American spirit, flags flying high, parades, and especially the fireworks. Every year, I like to invite my friends for a barbecue at my house with all of the fixin's.

I keep it casual and set up a big buffet and let everyone serve themselves. For decor, I keep with the Americana theme—lots of red, white, and blue. Once dessert has finished, I bring out the sparklers—a hit with the kids and the adults alike!

MENU

APL SHRIMP ON THE GRILL

ALL-AMERICAN POTATO SALAD

BBQ CHICKEN

KIWI-LILLET GIMLET

SUCCOTASH SALAD

STRAWBERRY FOOL

SERVES 8 TO 10

WINE

Gewürztraminer
Beaujolais

PLAYLIST

"Pink Houses" • BY JOHN MELLENCAMP
"Free Fallin'" • BY TOM PETTY
"Born to Run" • BY BRUCE SPRINGSTEEN
"Me and Bobby McGee" • BY JANIS JOPLIN
"American Pie" • BY DON MCLEAN

apl shrimp on the grill

This recipe is courtesy of my friend Adam Perry Lang. Adam is an incredible chef and has the *best* barbecue restaurant in New York City, called Daisy May's BBQ. Not only is he a great cook, but he's super nice. One afternoon, Adam and his wife Fleur came for lunch at my house. We were each cooking a dish and he whipped up this shrimp. This simple brining process makes the shrimp so succulent—you'll make this recipe over and over.

FOR THE BRINE

Combine the hot water, salt, and sugar in a large bowl. Stir until the sugar and salt dissolve. Add the cold water. Cut the lemons in half, squeeze the juice into the bowl, and add the lemons as well. Stir in the garlic, thyme, rosemary, and ice.

FOR THE SHRIMP

Working quickly, use a paring knife to cut along the curve of the back of the shrimp. Keep the shells intact. Remove the vein inside the shrimp and rinse gently with cold water. Place the shrimp in the brine as you go. Refrigerate the shrimp in the brine for 1 hour.

Brush the grill with oil and heat to medium. Combine the red pepper flakes and boiling water. Drain and discard the water. In a large bowl mix the olive oil, lemon juice, rehydrated red pepper flakes, and chives. Set aside.

Remove the shrimp from the brine and dry with paper towels. Toss the shrimp in the canola oil. Place the shrimp on the grill and cover with the lid. Grill for

continued

For the brine
1 CUP HOT WATER
1/4 CUP KOSHER SALT
2 TABLESPOONS SUGAR
7 CUPS COLD WATER
2 LEMONS
4 GARLIC CLOVES, GRATED ON A MICROPLANE
8 SPRIGS FRESH THYME, LIGHTLY CRUSHED
4 SPRIGS FRESH ROSEMARY, LIGHTLY CRUSHED
3 TO 4 CUPS ICE

For the shrimp
24 JUMBO (8 TO 12-COUNT) SHRIMP, SHELL-ON
1 TEASPOON RED PEPPER FLAKES
2 TABLESPOONS BOILING WATER
1/2 CUP EXTRA VIRGIN OLIVE OIL
JUICE OF 2 LEMONS
1/4 CUP MINCED CHIVES
1/3 CUP CANOLA OR VEGETABLE OIL
KOSHER SALT
FRESHLY GROUND COARSE BLACK PEPPER
COCKTAIL SAUCE WITH FRESH HORSE-RADISH, AND LEMON WEDGES, FOR SERVING

4 minutes. Turn the shrimp and cook another 4 minutes, until opaque. Remove from the grill and add to the olive oil mixture. Toss to coat and season with salt and pepper to taste. Serve with cocktail sauce and lemon wedges on the side.

8 TO 10 SERVINGS
PREP TIME: 30 MINUTES
INACTIVE PREP TIME: 1 HOUR
COOK TIME: 8 MINUTES

all-american potato salad

It wouldn't be summer without potato salad. When I was a kid, I never really liked it and I think it was because it always had too much stuff in it. I like my potato salad really simple: no pickles, eggs, or capers, just potatoes, scallions, and some herbs. If I'm making it for the Fourth of July, I like to use a combination of red, yellow, and blue potatoes for a patriotic touch.

Place the potatoes in a large pot and cover with salted water. Bring to a boil, reduce heat, cover, and cook until fork tender, about 30 minutes. Drain and cool completely. Slice the potatoes about ¼-inch thick.

In a large bowl, combine the mayonnaise, scallions, mustard, tarragon, parsley, lemon juice, salt, and pepper. Add the potatoes and toss gently to combine. Chill until serving time.

8 TO 10 SERVINGS
PREP TIME: 25 MINUTES
INACTIVE PREP TIME: 15 TO LET THE POTA-
    TOES COOL
COOK TIME: 30 MINUTES

3 POUNDS WHOLE SMALL ROUND
    POTATOES

½ CUP MAYONNAISE

¼ CUP CHOPPED SCALLIONS, WHITE
    AND GREEN PARTS

1 TABLESPOON DIJON MUSTARD

1 TABLESPOON MINCED FRESH
    TARRAGON

1 TABLESPOON MINCED FLAT-LEAF
    PARSLEY

JUICE OF 1 LEMON (ABOUT 3 TABLE-
    SPOONS)

1 TEASPOON KOSHER SALT

¼ TEASPOON FRESHLY GROUND
    BLACK PEPPER

bbq chicken

Barbecued chicken always makes me think of summertime. The sauce tickles all of the taste buds with both sweet and savory elements. My only complaint is that after cooking the chicken for so long on the grill, it tends to dry out. I decided to try cooking it partially on the grill and then transfer it to the oven. The chicken browns on the grill and takes on the smoky flavor and grill marks, and then I put it in a baking dish and cover it with sauce, and it braises at a low temperature until it is falling off the bone. You may need to make extra because people gobble this up like crazy!

FOR THE CHICKEN

In a small dish, combine the salt, chili powder, garlic powder, and black pepper. Season the chicken on both sides with this spice mixture. Drizzle with the olive oil. Cover and refrigerate for 1 to 2 hours.

FOR THE BBQ SAUCE

Heat the olive oil in a medium saucepan over medium heat. Sauté the onions until translucent, 7 to 8 minutes. Stir in the remaining ingredients. Bring to a low boil, reduce the heat to low, and simmer, stirring occasionally, for 30 minutes.

Meanwhile, preheat the oven to 350°F and heat the grill to medium-high.

Brush the grill with oil. Place the chicken skin side down and cook 5 minutes. Turn and cook an additional 5 minutes. Place the chicken in a baking dish in one layer. Pour the BBQ sauce over the chicken. Cover tightly with

For the chicken

2 TABLESPOONS KOSHER SALT

2 TEASPOONS CHILI POWDER

1 TEASPOON GARLIC POWDER

1 TEASPOON FRESHLY GROUND BLACK PEPPER

2 CHICKENS (EACH CUT IN 10 PIECES, BACKBONE REMOVED)

2 TABLESPOONS OLIVE OIL

For the BBQ sauce

1 TABLESPOON OLIVE OIL

1 CUP MINCED YELLOW ONION

2 CUPS KETCHUP

¾ CUP LOW-SODIUM CHICKEN BROTH

¼ CUP APPLE CIDER VINEGAR

¼ CUP DARK BROWN SUGAR

¼ CUP MOLASSES

1 TABLESPOON WORCESTERSHIRE SAUCE

1 TABLESPOON CHILI POWDER

1 TEASPOON GARLIC POWDER

continued

For the BBQ sauce (continued)
1 TEASPOON SMOKED PAPRIKA

⅛ TEASPOON CAYENNE PEPPER

1 TEASPOON DRY MUSTARD

1 TEASPOON GROUND CUMIN

1 TEASPOON GROUND CORIANDER

aluminum foil. Bake for 45 minutes, until fork tender.

8 TO 10 SERVINGS
PREP TIME: 15 MINUTES
INACTIVE PREP TIME: 1 TO 2 HOURS
COOK TIME: 10 MINUTES ON THE GRILL AND
   45 MINUTES IN THE OVEN

TIP

If using this sauce for the Broiled Spicy Tofu (page 180), make it vegetarian-friendly by substituting vegetable broth for chicken broth.

kiwi-lillet gimlet

A couple of years ago, a friend brought me a bottle of Lillet. It quickly became my favorite summer drink, just poured over ice with a splash of soda. I started experimenting and came up with this spin on a gimlet. The frozen kiwi looks so pretty in the glass and the mint and gin make it very refreshing on a hot day. Be careful—it goes down easy!

Freeze the kiwi in a single layer on a sheet pan lined with parchment paper.

In a pitcher, combine the Lillet, club soda, gin, and mint. Add frozen kiwi and 2 cups of ice. Serve in highball glasses.

2 KIWIS, PEELED AND SLICED

4 CUPS LILLET BLONDE

$\frac{1}{2}$ CUP CLUB SODA

$\frac{1}{4}$ CUP GIN

FRESH MINT LEAVES

2 CUPS ICE

8 TO 10 SERVINGS (ABOUT 5 CUPS)
PREP TIME: 5 MINUTES
INACTIVE PREP TIME: ABOUT 1 HOUR TO
    FREEZE KIWIS

succotash salad

This salad looks so pretty and colorful, kind of like confetti made of the colors of summer. I like to make it ahead of time to allow the vegetables some time to marinate. It is great left over the next day as well. I also make this in the winter sometimes and use frozen vegetables.

CORN CUT FROM 6 EARS, ABOUT 4
  CUPS

ONE 16-OUNCE PACKAGE FROZEN
  LIMA BEANS, THAWED

2 CUPS BLANCHED GREEN BEANS,
  CUT INTO 1-INCH PIECES

1 CUP GRAPE TOMATOES, SLICED
  LENGTHWISE

½ CUP MINCED RED ONION

1 AVOCADO, PITTED, PEELED, AND
  CUT INTO CHUNKS

1 JALAPEÑO, SEEDED AND MINCED

10 BASIL LEAVES, CHIFFONADED

½ CUP EXTRA VIRGIN OLIVE OIL

¼ CUP RED WINE VINEGAR

1 TEASPOON HONEY

1 TEASPOON KOSHER SALT

½ TEASPOON FRESHLY GROUND
  BLACK PEPPER

In a large bowl, combine the corn, lima beans, green beans, tomatoes, onions, avocado, jalapeño, and basil. In a separate bowl, whisk the oil, vinegar, honey, salt, and pepper. Add the vinaigrette to the salad and toss to coat.

8 TO 10 SERVINGS
PREP TIME: 20 MINUTES
COOK TIME: 4 MINUTES TO BLANCH GREEN
  BEANS

strawberry fool

There's nothing foolish about this old-fashioned classic dessert. It is creamy and delicious and takes no time at all to prepare. I like to serve it with some shortbread cookies on the side.

2 CUPS SLICED STRAWBERRIES

1/2 CUP SUGAR

2 TABLESPOONS FRESH LEMON JUICE

2 CUPS HEAVY CREAM

MINT LEAVES, FOR GARNISH

In a blender, combine strawberries (reserve a few slices for garnish), sugar, and lemon juice. Puree until smooth. Push berry mixture through a sieve and discard seeds.

Using an electric mixer, whip the cream just until stiff peaks form. Take a large spoonful of the whipped cream and stir it into the strawberry puree to lighten the mix. Fold the strawberry mixture gently into the whipped cream. Gently spoon the fool into a chilled serving bowl and garnish with the reserved sliced strawberries and mint leaves. Refrigerate before serving, up to 4 hours.

8 TO 10 SERVINGS
PREP TIME: 15 MINUTES
INACTIVE PREP TIME: AT LEAST 1 HOUR

beach picnic

Summer in the Hamptons means picnic time. Almost every weekend, I head to the beach with my friends. I'm always in charge of the food and I like to get creative with our menus. I steer clear of the usual ham and cheese sandwiches and mayonnaise-based salads, and instead opt to keep it light and clean with foods that won't spoil quickly in the summer heat.

If you don't live near the beach, head to a local park or even have a picnic in your own backyard. And please don't be a litterbug!

MENU

CHILLED CANTALOUPE AND MINT SOUP

MARINATED VEGETABLE SANDWICHES
WITH GOAT CHEESE AND PESTO

AVOCADO, RADISH, AND GRAPE QUINOA
SALAD

STRAWBERRY HAND PIES

CRANBERRY-LIME ROSÉ SPRITZER

SERVES 4

WINE

Sofia Minis
(sparkling wine that
comes in a can)

PLAYLIST

"The Fear" • BY LILY ALLEN
"Friday I'm in Love" • BY THE CURE
"Time to Pretend" • BY MGMT
"Under Pressure" • BY DAVID BOWIE AND QUEEN
"I Don't Feel Like Dancing" • BY THE SCISSOR SISTERS

For the Picnic Basket and Cooler

LARGE BLANKET

PILLOWS OR CUSHIONS

ECO-FRIENDLY PLATES AND FLATWARE

DISHTOWELS
(serve as placemat and napkin)

SPEAKERS FOR YOUR IPOD

GAMES
(like backgammon and a deck of cards)

TRASH BAGS
(one for trash and one for recyclables)

SUNSCREEN

BUG SPRAY

WET WIPES

chilled cantaloupe and mint soup

Even on the hottest day of the year, this soup is guaranteed to cool you down and revitalize your energy level. When I'm preparing for a picnic, I divide the soup into individual servings in jars with tight-fitting lids and pack them in the cooler. Everyone gets their own jar and can just sip the soup, rather than needing a spoon. The pale orange color of the cantaloupe with the bright green flecks of mint looks as refreshing as it tastes.

1 CANTALOUPE, SEEDS AND RIND REMOVED, CUT INTO CHUNKS

2 TABLESPOONS MINCED FRESH MINT

JUICE OF 1 LIME

PINCH OF SALT

In a blender, combine all ingredients and blend until smooth. Pour into a sealable container and chill for at least 3 hours and up to overnight. Shake well and pour into serving dishes.

4 SERVINGS
PREP TIME: 10 MINUTES
INACTIVE PREP TIME: AT LEAST 3 HOURS
    AND UP TO OVERNIGHT

marinated vegetable sandwiches with goat cheese and pesto

This vegetable sandwich is packed with flavor. I use zucchini, eggplant, squash, and mushrooms, but experiment with whatever vegetables look good at your local farm stand.

FOR THE VEGETABLES

In a small bowl, combine the olive oil, lemon juice, Worcestershire, thyme, garlic powder, onion powder, salt, and pepper. Whisk until emulsified.

Place the zucchini, eggplant, squash, and mushrooms in a sealable container or resealable plastic bag. Pour the marinade over the vegetables and toss to combine. Refrigerate at least 3 hours and up to overnight, tossing vegetables once or twice.

FOR THE SANDWICHES

Slice baguette into four equal parts. Split the bread horizontally, then spread one side of each sandwich with 1 tablespoon of goat cheese and the other side with 1 tablespoon pesto. Set aside.

Heat a grill pan over medium heat. Remove vegetables from marinade and cook for 3 to 4 minutes on each side. Place the roasted vegetables on the bread. Can be served immediately or wrapped and served a few hours later.

4 SERVINGS
PREP TIME: 20 MINUTES
INACTIVE PREP TIME: 3 HOURS OR UP TO
   OVERNIGHT
COOK TIME: 10 MINUTES

For the vegetables
¼ CUP EXTRA VIRGIN OLIVE OIL

JUICE OF 2 LEMONS

1 TABLESPOON WORCESTERSHIRE
   SAUCE

1 TEASPOON FRESH THYME LEAVES

¼ TEASPOON GARLIC POWDER

¼ TEASPOON ONION POWDER

¾ TEASPOON KOSHER SALT

¼ TEASPOON FRESHLY GROUND
   BLACK PEPPER

2 ZUCCHINI, THINLY SLICED
   LENGTHWISE

2 JAPANESE EGGPLANT, THINLY
   SLICED LENGTHWISE

1 YELLOW SQUASH, THINLY SLICED
   LENGTHWISE

2 PORTOBELLO MUSHROOM CAPS,
   THINLY SLICED

For the sandwiches
1 BAGUETTE

¼ CUP GOAT CHEESE, AT ROOM TEM-
   PERATURE

¼ CUP PESTO (STORE-BOUGHT OR
   HOMEMADE)

avocado, radish, and grape quinoa salad

In my last cookbook, I had a recipe for a sugar snap pea and radish salad. Time and again, people would tell me that it was one of their favorites. I think it's because of the balance of the peppery radishes with the sweet snap peas. Here I've combined radishes with grapes and avocados. I love the way it tastes, but also the texture next to the grainy quinoa is fantastic, not to mention really healthy.

1 CUP QUINOA

$\frac{1}{3}$ CUP EXTRA VIRGIN OLIVE OIL

1 SHALLOT, MINCED

$\frac{1}{4}$ TEASPOON GROUND CUMIN

$\frac{1}{4}$ CUP FRESH LEMON JUICE

$1\frac{1}{4}$ TEASPOONS KOSHER SALT

$\frac{3}{4}$ TEASPOON FRESHLY GROUND
BLACK PEPPER

1 AVOCADO

1 BUNCH RADISHES, THINLY SLICED
(ABOUT 1 CUP)

$\frac{1}{2}$ CUP RED GRAPES, SLICED IN HALF

$\frac{1}{4}$ CUP CHIFFONADED FRESH BASIL
(FROM ABOUT 8 LEAVES)

Cook the quinoa according to package instructions. Set aside to cool completely.

In a small dish, whisk the olive oil, shallot, cumin, 3 tablespoons lemon juice, the salt, and pepper until emulsified. Cover and reserve.

Cut the avocado in half, remove the pit, and scoop out the flesh. Cut each half in thin slices and drizzle with the remaining lemon juice.

In a large bowl, combine the quinoa, radishes, grapes, avocado, and basil. Pour the vinaigrette over the salad and toss gently to combine. Refrigerate until serving time.

4 SERVINGS
PREP TIME: 15 MINUTES
INACTIVE PREP TIME: 20 MINUTES TO COOL
    QUINOA
COOK TIME: ABOUT 20 MINUTES

strawberry hand pies

Mmmmm—strawberry pie! So good, but too messy for a picnic. With these hand pies, you get the same effect without the mess, and they are so much more fun! Kids love these and so do adults. They also freeze perfectly.

Preheat the oven to 375°F.

In a small saucepan over medium heat, combine the strawberries, flour, sugar, and lemon zest. Cook about 10 minutes, until mixture thickens, stirring often. Set aside to cool.

On a lightly floured surface, use a rolling pin to roll out the circles of pastry dough. Cut the edges of each to form a large square. Cut each into quarters. Place 4 on greased baking sheet. Spoon the strawberry mixture onto four of the squares, leaving a border around the edges. Brush edges with egg and top with another square. Use a fork to seal the edges and create a decorative border. In the center of the hand pie, use fork to create a vent. Brush with milk and sprinkle with sugar.

Bake 30 minutes, rotating once, until golden brown. Cool on a wire rack.

4 SERVINGS
PREP TIME: 20 MINUTES
INACTIVE PREP TIME: 15 MINUTES TO COOL
    STRAWBERRY FILLING
COOK TIME: 30 MINUTES

2 CUPS SLICED FRESH STRAW-
    BERRIES (ABOUT 1 POUND)

2 TABLESPOONS ALL-PURPOSE
    FLOUR

½ CUP SUGAR, PLUS MORE FOR
    SPRINKLING

1 TEASPOON GRATED LEMON ZEST

2 CIRCLES REFRIGERATED PIE
    DOUGH (HOMEMADE OR IF STORE
    BOUGHT, NOT IN A PIE DISH—I
    USE PILLSBURY)

1 EGG, LIGHTLY BEATEN

1 TABLESPOON MILK

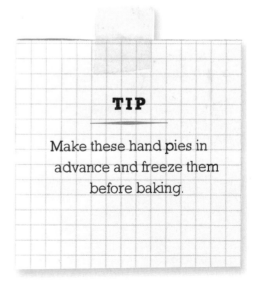

TIP

Make these hand pies in advance and freeze them before baking.

cranberry-lime rosé spritzer

In the summer, I buy rosé wine by the case and somehow I'm still always running out of it. My friends drink it like Kool-Aid. To make it go further, I created these spritzers. They are so light, and the effervescence from the seltzer water makes for a refreshing summer cocktail. For a picnic, make it at home and pack it in a sealable carafe.

1 BOTTLE ROSÉ WINE

2 CUPS SELTZER WATER

1 CUP NO-SUGAR-ADDED
    CRANBERRY JUICE

JUICE OF 1 LIME

$\frac{1}{4}$ CUP SUPERFINE SUGAR

1 LIME, THINLY SLICED

Pour the rosé, seltzer, cranberry juice, lime juice, and sugar into a pitcher. Stir until the sugar is dissolved. Stir in lime slices. Chill until serving time.

4 SERVINGS
PREP TIME: 5 MINUTES
INACTIVE PREP TIME: AT LEAST 20 MINUTES
    TO CHILL

ACKNOWLEDGMENTS

Thank you so much to my lovely cookbook team—gifted photographer Miki Duisterhof, food stylist extraordinaire Paul Lowe, the incredibly chic prop stylist Kim Ficaro, the glam squad Julie Tussey and Marc Mena, and the ever-diligent recipe tester Katrina Norwood.

On the publishing side, I couldn't ask for a better group—the ever-enthusiastic Jennifer Bergstrom, the meticulous Tricia Boczkowski, and the dynamic duo of design, Michael Nagin and Jane Archer.

My super-smart posse at William Morris Endeavor—Andy McNicol, Jon Rosen, Jason Hodes, and Jeff Googel, and my brilliant publicist Keleigh Thomas and the team at Sunshine Sachs.

Lots of love to my friends who spent time posing for pictures—Marcy Blum, Gretta Monahan, Fabiola Beracasa, Nate Berkus, Brian Atwood, and my loving taste testers Mark Mullet, Keith Bloomfield, and Bill.

A very, very special thank you to my dear friend Anne Thornton (aka Patsy), who was there every single day of the photo shoot and supported me all the way through the writing, testing, and editing process.

INDEX